TEN GIRLS
WHO CHANGED
THE WORLD

LIGHT KEEPERS

Irene Howat

CF4·K

Copyright © Christian Focus Publications 2001
This revised edition printed 2001
Reprinted 2002, 2003 twice, 2004, 2005, 2006, 2007,
2008, 2009, 2010, 2011, 2013, 2014, 2015, 2016, 2020, 2022
Paperback ISBN: 978-1-85792-649-1
E-pub ISBN: 978-1-84550-848-7
Mobi ISBN: 978-1-84550-849-4

Published by Christian Focus Publications, Geanies House, Fearn,
Tain, Ross-shire, IV20 1TW, Scotland, Great Britain
www.christianfocus.com
email:info@christianfocus.com
Cover design by Alister MacInnes.
Cover illustration by Elena Temporin,
Milan Illustrations Agency.
Printed and bound in China

All incidents retold in these stories are based on true situations. Where specific information about childhood incidents has been unobtainable the author has written these paragraphs using other information concerning family life, hobbies, homelife, relationships freely available in other biographies as well as appropriate historical source material.

Front cover: As a young girl growing up in The Netherlands, Corrie ten Boom lived with her father, mother and sister, Betsie, in a little watch shop in Haarlem, a fifteen minute train ride west of Amsterdam. Corrie herself went on to be one of the first qualified female watchmakers in The Netherlands. During the second world war her home was used as a refuge for Jewish people on the run from the Nazi authorities. Corrie and her sister were later imprisoned in a concentration camp. Betsie died but Corrie survived to tell their story.

For
Georgia Holly

Contents

Isobel Kuhn

Isobel and her brother sat in the tree-house in their garden, waiting and watching for their parents' visitors to arrive.

'They've come all the way from China,' Isobel said. 'I guess they'll have lots of interesting stories to tell us.'

Both the children loved stories and looked forward to visitors coming from interesting faraway places. As she also loved telling stories, Isobel told her brother a story as they waited for their visitors to arrive.

'A long time ago and a long way away there were two missionaries whose names were Paul and Barnabas. One day they saw a man who had never walked in all of his life. When the man looked up Paul told him to stand on his feet. Guess what the man did?'

'Did he tell Paul that he couldn't do that?' asked the boy.

'No, he didn't,' Isobel told him. 'The man jumped up and began to walk!'

Her brother was wide-eyed.

'That's a miracle,' he announced.

Isabel agreed. 'And as that story is in the Bible we know it's true,' she added.

Just then a little group of people arrived at the gate.

'Shoosh!' Isobel whispered. 'There they are.'

The pair of them clambered down the tree and ran towards the house.

'Do you never get tired of all the missionaries Dad invites home?' the boy asked breathlessly.

Isobel grinned. 'No, and I never get tired of telling stories either!'

Isobel and her brother soon realised that these visitors weren't really that different to them. The brother and sister climbed down the tree to run to meet and greet their visitors from another country.

They were soon running about and playing together just like children the world over.

'They've come all the way from China,' Isobel marvelled. 'I wonder what that must be like?'

When Isobel Miller (that was what she was called before she married) went to university, she decided that she didn't believe in God. That made her father and mother very sad. They prayed for her, asking God to show their daughter how much she needed the Saviour. It took some years, but eventually their prayers were answered. Isobel, who was by then a teacher, discovered for herself that believing in Jesus and trusting in him is not dull and boring and only for old people. It made her happier than she had ever been before.

At a conference Isobel heard a missionary speak about his work with the Lisu people in China. As he was speaking, she longed to go there and to tell these people about the Lord Jesus.

'We need men to work with the Lisu,' the speaker said, as he finished his talk.

'I wonder if they need women too?' Isobel thought to herself.

Someone she met at that conference paid for Isobel to go to Bible College in America and it was there that she met John Kuhn. He was also training to be a missionary, and he too felt God wanted him to go to China.

John, who was a year ahead of Isobel at College, finished his course and left for the mission field. They were by then very much in love. How Isobel missed him.

It wasn't until nearly two years later, in October 1928, that Isobel boarded a ship at Vancouver dock and set sail for China and her husband-to-be. But it was a long time until the Kuhns went from the great plains of China to work with the Lisu people in the faraway mountains and by then they had a little daughter, Kathryn. Isobel could hardly believe it when they eventually arrived in Lisuland!

'Jesus loves me, this I know,
for the Bible tells me so,'

Kathryn sang to her friends in the language of the Lisu. 'Now you sing.' Six smiling dark-eyed children sang along with her.

'Little ones to him belong.
They are weak but he is strong.'

Her mother's voice joined in,

'Yes, Jesus loves me,
the Bible tells me so.'

'Lord,' Isobel prayed. 'Thank you that even Kathryn is a missionary here. Please let these little children really hear what she's saying and learn that you love them.'

When the Kuhns were in Lisuland, China and Japan were at war. Sometimes soldiers came to the village they lived in and made the people very afraid. When the time came for John and Isobel to go home on leave and introduce little Kathryn to her family in Canada and America, they were sorry to go, because it came at a bad time for the Lisu people. But their home leave soon passed and they set out again for China, despite the Second World War making travel hazardous.

'There's a telegram for you,' John was told when their boat called at Hong Kong.

His wife watched as he opened it. 'Was it bad news from home?' she wondered.

'Send Kathryn to Chefoo with Grace Liddell,' John read.

Isobel's face turned white. 'But that means saying goodbye to her here and now!'

The Kuhns had expected Kathryn to go away to school when they arrived back in China but now the mission was instructing them to send her with another missionary who was travelling to a mission school in what is now Malaysia. They weren't even going to be in the same country!

There were very sad farewells but everyone tried to be brave. Thankfully John and Isobel didn't know that Chefoo School would soon be captured by the Japanese and that it would be a very long time before they even received a letter from Kathryn to say that she was safe and well. Isobel broke her heart when Kathryn left and it took a while before she lost her deep sadness.

'I wonder what's the best way to make an impact on these mountain villages?' John thought aloud, as he and Isobel talked in their hut one evening soon after their return to Lisuland.

'Well, one thing's sure,' his wife said, 'we can't be in them all at once.'

There was a silence.

'I've been thinking,' her husband went on. 'The best way forward would be to train the young Christians to be missionaries to their own people.'

'But how do we do that? They can't come here one day a week for classes because some of them live four days' walk away,' Isobel pointed out. 'They can't come in the dry season because they've got to work in the fields. And it's not safe to travel in the rainy season, it's too easy to slip on the mountain paths. Every year that happens and people are killed.'

'I was wondering,' John continued, 'if we could have a Rainy Season Bible School. The young men could come before the rains made walking dangerous, stay here and study until the worst of the rain had passed and it was safe to go home again.'

Isobel's eyes lit up. 'That's a wonderful idea!'

John grinned. 'Thank you, I think so too!'

The Rainy Season Bible School was born, and it was a great success. Young men came from long distances to study the Bible. Each weekend during the Bible School they went to nearby villages where they preached and taught the children.

At the end of their studies they went back to their homes and told the people there about the Lord God.

Having seen the success of the boys' Bible School, Isobel decided to have one for girls too. The men in the church just laughed at the idea. They thought girls didn't have enough brains to learn things from books!

John was working in another part of China when the first Bible School for girls was held. Isobel wrote to tell him about it.

'Twenty-two girls attended,' she wrote. 'We held tests and gave out certificates to those who passed. The results were good. One even got first-class honours.

Can you guess who that was?

It was the blind girl from Mountain Top Village! I asked her how she had learned her Bible passages. She smiled as she told me.

"I could hear the other girls in my hut going over their notes and learning their verses, so I studied by listening to them." '

During the Bible School, some of the girls held a Sunday School in the village the Kuhns lived in.

But every time Isobel heard the children singing 'Jesus loves me' she thought about her own little girlie and prayed that she was safe and that God was caring for the missionary children at Chefoo.

'Ohh ... Ohh ...' Isobel moaned in her sleep. 'My tooth is so sore.'

John didn't hear her. He was hundreds of miles away on mission business.

The tooth was no better in the morning and the pain grew dreadfully as time passed. The nearest dentist was two weeks' journey away but eventually the missionary decided that she had to go.

A young Lisu man went with Isobel to keep her company, and to protect her as soldiers and bandits were making the area unsafe for travel.

'I'll meet up with John and we can come home together,' she told her companion.

But the war between China and Japan caught up with her and it was months before she and her husband were back in the village. Something else caught up with Isobel too, a letter from Kathryn saying that the Japanese were looking after the schoolchildren well and that there was no need to worry.

'I'm so glad that tooth brought me to the town,' she told a missionary friend. 'If I'd still been in the village I probably wouldn't have got Kathryn's letter.'

After that, regular letters got through to Chefoo and one was full of lovely news.

'My dear girlie,' Isobel wrote, 'you're now a big sister! Little Danny was born yesterday and I'm writing right away so that you'll know the news as soon as you possibly can.

Your brother has tiny ears, just like sea shells. His eyes are like deep pools of water.

I've checked his fingers and toes, and he has ten of each of them. He is such a cutie, just like you were when you were born.'

When Kathryn got the letter, she wrote back immediately.

'I can't believe that I really have a baby brother! It's the bestest news I could possibly get. I was working it out, and if everything goes as we've planned, I'll see Danny when he's just a year old. He'll still be a bit of a baby then, won't he? I do want to see him while he's still a baby. Ask someone who's artistic to draw me a picture of Danny. I'd just LOVE to see him.'

For Kathryn that year passed slowly. As she was now in her teens, she travelled to America with some missionaries who were returning home. When she arrived she was looked after by another Christian family who became a sort of foster family to her.

'I can't wait for the family to come,' she told her friends. 'I've never even met my baby brother.'

John, Isobel and Danny were on their way to America. It was a dangerous journey because the Second World War was still raging and ships didn't always arrive at their destinations. Many were torpedoed as they crossed the oceans. But God looked after the little missionary family and they met with each other at last, the first time ever all four of them had been together.

'Allo Kafin,' Danny said, a little shyly at first.

Kathryn held out her arms to her baby brother.

The toddler looked at his mum, then at his dad, and saw they were smiling. So he walked unsteadily to his sister, held up his arms and snuggled into her neck when she lifted him. Kathryn was glad the little boy could not see her face. She was crying, crying tears of joy and delight.

For over a year John and Isobel, Kathryn and Danny lived a normal family life. Because they had been so often separated, that was very special to them.

Kathryn got to know her parents again, for she had grown up in the time they'd been apart. And she got to know Danny, who thought having a big sister was a splendid thing.

But the day came when they had to say 'goodbye' again, and Kathryn waved the family off on their long journey back to China. It was a heartbreaking time for Isobel and John Kuhn and their daughter Kathryn.

Kathryn stayed in America because of her education. But despite all the times that being missionaries had meant that her family were countries apart from each other, when Kathryn Kuhn decided what she would do with her life, she felt that God wanted her to be a missionary too.

The years of separation the Kuhn family had undergone didn't discourage their eldest daughter from a life of missionary service for her God. She knew what to expect and decided that she wanted to give her life to God and to telling people about him and his son, Jesus Christ.

Eventually Isobel Kuhn was forced to leave the mission field and return to life in America. Her health was poor and she could no longer stay with the Lisu people she loved so much. Mission work was now out of the question. Isobel needed urgent surgery that she could only receive in the United States. But it meant being reunited with Kathryn and Danny. Both Isobel's children were by then living in America.

And one day Isobel Kuhn waved goodbye to another young woman who was heading off to the other side of the world as a missionary, just as she had done many years before. As they took their last farewells, Isobel wiped a tear from her eye and breathed a sigh of relief. It was good to realise that all the separation, heartache and suffering hadn't harmed Kathryn too much. Isobel's little girlie had grown up and she too was leaving to become a missionary, a missionary in China!

That evening Isobel thought back to all her years in China. Then her eye caught sight of the books she had written about the Lisu people since her return to America. She picked up her pen. Isobel knew she hadn't long to live, but she still had work to do.

Isobel Kuhn died and went home to Jesus in 1957.

FACT FILE

Posting a letter - mail used to be delivered by hand. You would either employ someone to deliver your letter for you or send it with a travelling friend. It was a very expensive and unreliable system.

The postage stamp was invented in 1840. It is really a receipt to show that you have paid a fee for the letter to be delivered by the Post Office.

When Isobel was in China, mail would take months to arrive. Today, a letter can be sent by airmail to China in a matter of days and an e-mail in a matter of minutes.

Keynote: Isobel and her family were often apart from one another. It was always very difficult to say goodbye, but it was a comfort to know that God was with them all.

Learn from Isobel's experience that as a Christian you are never alone. Jesus promises never to leave you.

Think: Have you ever thought about writing a letter to a missionary? Getting news from home and some encouraging words will mean so much to a missionary who is far away from family and friends.

Prayer: Lord Jesus, thank you for missionaries who leave their homes, families and friends to bring the message of Jesus to people who have never heard about you.

Comfort them when they are lonely and be with those at home who miss them most. Amen.

Elizabeth Fry

The child screwed up her face and looked in the mirror. "Am I beautiful?" she asked herself. So many beautiful ladies came to see her Mama that sometimes Elizabeth's home, Earlham Hall near Norwich, seemed as though it were lived in by butterflies rather than people. The ladies wore long dresses in every colour of silk, dresses that rustled as they moved. And when they brushed against her she loved to feel their cool softness.

'I can't wait to be a lady,' she told her reflection. 'I'll wear the most splendid dresses of all.'

'Have you finished brushing your hair, Miss Elizabeth?' her maid Jane, asked.

The girl jumped. She had forgotten why she was in front of the mirror!

'You help me,' she said. 'My arm gets tired with all the brushing.'

'How many have you done?' asked the woman.

Elizabeth was torn between honesty and her dislike of having her long hair brushed. Honesty won. 'None.'

Taking the brush in one hand and loosening the child's hair with the other, Jane started to count, one for each long stroke. 'One, two, three ...,' till after what seemed a very long time, 'ninety eight, ninety nine, a hundred.'

With a deep sigh the woman laid down the brush. 'Sometimes I wish your hair wasn't quite so long,' she said. 'It hurts my poor back to bend down so far.'

The child swung round, her hair swirling behind her. 'Dance with me,' she said. 'Let's pretend we are at one of Papa and Mama's great parties.'

Elizabeth's maid laughed, bowed to her young partner, then danced one of the formal dances of the day with her.

When she was being tucked up in bed that night, Elizabeth looked thoughtful.

'A penny for your thoughts,' Jane said.

'I was wondering what I'll be doing in the year 1800. That's ten years from now and I'll be twenty years old. I'll have fine silk dresses and I'll go to a party every week and I'll dance with the handsomest of all the young men. Do you think I'll do all that when I'm twenty?'

The maid folded over her linen sheet and tucked in the blankets. 'What I think is this,' she said, 'tomorrow is Sunday and you'd best be thinking about Sunday things not about parties and all.'

Elizabeth Gurney closed her eyes until the door was shut then opened them again. She loved watching the coal fire in the nursery after her candle was blown out.

'Sunday,' she thought. 'Why are there so many Sundays. They are not nearly such fun as other days. The services at the Friends' Meeting House are so long. And the sermons are so boring, boring that I run out of things to think about!'

She turned on to her side, closed her eyes and tired to forget that tomorrow was Sunday.

By the year 1800 Elizabeth felt differently. Three years earlier, when she was seventeen years old she heard an American preacher, William Savery, and learned from him that Jesus died to save her from her sins. She was thrilled by what she heard and trusted her heart to the Lord. And, some months afterwards, when she was told at a Quaker meeting (her family were from a well known and very wealthy Quaker family) that she would be, 'a light to the blind, speech to the dumb and feet to the lame, Elizabeth felt sure that God had special work for her to do. From then on she kept herself busy doing good where she saw any kind of need.

'Will you miss the work you do?' Joseph Fry, Elizabeth's fiancé, asked her just before they were to be married when she was twenty years old.

She nodded. 'I think I may, but I can't take my Sunday School class to London with me, and I don't expect I'll have time to make clothes for the poor. I'll be so busy running our home.'

'I think you will,' Joseph smiled. 'But may I ask you something?'

Elizabeth looked up sharply. 'Is there anything wrong?'

'Not at all. I was just wondering if you'll continue to wear Plain Quaker clothes when you come to the capital.'

The lovely young woman looked down at her simple grey wool dress and put her hand up to touch her grey bonnet. 'Yes,' she said gently. 'Yes, I believe I will. I don't think the Lord means me to be dressed like a showy parrot in all sorts of bright colours. It would just draw attention to myself and that doesn't seem right.'

Elizabeth wore Plain Quaker clothes for the rest of her life. The women of the Quaker group in which she had been brought up had no restriction of what they wore, the more glamorous they were the better and their social diaries were full. Plain Quakers were different, they lived quietly and simply and dressed in the plainest of clothes. When she remembered back to her childhood dreams, the new Mrs Fry smiled and shook her head.

She was busy after she was married, but it wasn't a business that satisfied her. So, when eight years later in 1808 Elizabeth and her husband moved to Plashet in Essex, she was more than ready to find some useful things to do in the community. First she employed a teacher and set up a school. Then she organised a place where poor people could have a bowl of hot soup. And when she heard people in the neighbourhood were sick, she visited them, taking a basketful of good things with her. In those days if men were ill and could not work no money came into the house at all. Families were sometimes in real danger of starving. Elizabeth Fry did all that she could to help when she heard of hardship of any kind.

It was 1813, and Elizabeth Fry was speaking urgently to a group of women, all dressed as simply as she was.

'I've called you together to tell you about Mr Stephen Grellet, the American Quaker.'

The women were interested, a visitor from the other side of the Atlantic Ocean was still unusual.

'He took the opportunity to visit Newgate Prison and was shocked by what he found. There are women and children as well as men locked up in that place. Apparently it is filthy and smells disgusting.'

'What can we do?' one of the company asked.

'We should do something,' another said.

'We must go there,' Elizabeth told them.

'We must go and see for ourselves what can be done.'

'Could we take clothing with us?'

'And blankets?'

'Some nourishing food will be needed, I'm sure.'

What started as Elizabeth telling about Newgate Prison turned into a planning meeting with its sole topic how to change things there. With her group of Quaker ladies, Elizabeth Fry went to the prison carrying bundles and bags and baskets. The conditions shocked them. Even women and children slept on the floor with only a thin layer of rotten straw underneath them. Before leaving, the ladies paid the turnkey (the jailor) to replace the straw regularly. The women in the prison must have wondered if they would ever see their visitors again, or had they just come as a one-off effort at helping. If that's what they thought they were wrong.

Newgate Prison held three hundred women and children in just four rooms. All they did, they did there: cooking, eating, sleeping and everything else as well. Each day the women and men were allowed to mix together and Elizabeth was appalled that their time was spent gambling and drinking, fighting and dancing. It wasn't a pleasant atmosphere and certainly not one for young children, and there were many children there. Not all of the prisoners were guilty of a crime, many were just there awaiting trial. And those who were criminals came out worse than when they went in.

'It's that Quaker lady,' one woman prisoner said to another when Elizabeth next visited. 'It's taken her years to come back. I thought we'd never see her again.'

'Wot kept ye?' she yelled, when Mrs Fry was shown into the dark and smelly room.

Elizabeth explained that for the four years since her last visit she had been unable to give time to much else but her family. But now she intended doing something about their prison conditions.

'Wot are ye gonna do?' a women said from the corner where she was nursing her baby. An older boy and girl cuddled in beside her.

'First of all I hope to start a school for these children,' Mrs Fry explained. 'They shouldn't be here at all and the least we can do is give them schooling.'

'A school!'

'In here!'

A thin woman brought her skinny little girl to the visitor. 'Will you take my Ann for a pupil?'

Elizabeth smiled at the dirty child.

'Yes,' she said. 'She'll be the school's very first pupil.'

It wasn't long until the school was running and mothers were offering help with it. Others wanted to be taught themselves.

'Are you serious?' Elizabeth asked.

Several heads nodded eagerly.

'What do you want to be taught?'

'Sewing,' said one, 'then I'll be able to earn some money when I get out of here.'

'Knitting,' another suggested. 'My little Cathy needs warm clothes for the winter. It's freezing in here come October.'

'And we could sell what we make,' one bright young woman added. 'Then we could buy things the children need. I want my John to have shoes this winter. Last year he cried himself to sleep every night because of his chilblains.'

There was no shortage of suggestions, and Elizabeth was not short of enthusiasm. Soon several classes of twelve women were set up, each doing a different craft. And Mrs Fry opened a shop in the prison where the women could buy things with the little money they earned. A group of her Quaker friends joined with her and at least one of them visited the prison every single day.

At 9am and 6pm each day Elizabeth went to Newgate to take a short service. She didn't only preach to the women, she helped them in all sorts of other ways too. Many prisoners were moved by what she said, especially as she didn't only preach to them she helped them in practical ways too. Her prison work became so well known that committees like her one were set up all over the country to help women in prisons just as bad as Newgate. And the news of what was happening there travelled further still, and so did Elizabeth. She went as far as Russia telling people about the need to do something about prison conditions.

'I can hardly take in what you're saying!' Elizabeth Fry gasped when, in 1818, she heard for the first time about the evils of transportation. 'Tell me exactly what's happening.'

The man took a deep breath and began. 'A convict can be transported to the colonies for life if he steals an apron or a side of bacon. And for taking half a kilo of potatoes or a pair of shoes he can be sent away for fourteen years.'

'They are sent half way round the world! What happens to the women?' she asked.

'They are chained together and carried to the ships in open carts.'

Her eyes opened wide.

'And when they get to the colonies they're treated no better than slaves. They're given nowhere to stay and no decent work to do.'

'I must do something about this,' Elizabeth said. 'Indeed, I really must.'

It didn't take long for Elizabeth to persuade the Governor of Newgate to treat the transports better. By then he knew that his prison visitor meant business. In any case, the women in prison were much less trouble since the school and craft classes started. But Elizabeth didn't just stop at changing things for the Newgate transports. She took her complaint right to the government and made sure the Members of Parliament listened to her too. As a result of her campaign women transports were given proper places to stay and work to do when they reached the colonies.

For the next twenty five years Elizabeth Fry checked when convict ships sailing from London docks were to be carrying women, and she visited them with a Bible and sewing kit for each woman. A total of 126 ships with 12,000 prisoners left London docks over that time. But, thanks mainly to Elizabeth, the number of people transported began to go down and by 1854 no more people were sent to the faraway colonies at all.

'You've done wonders over the years,' a friend told Elizabeth, when they were both quite elderly women.

Mrs Fry shook her head. 'I could have done so much more,' she said.

Her friend spoke a little crossly. 'What else could you have done? As well as all your work for prison reform you've opened a night shelter for the homeless, founded a Nurses' training home, not to mention all the District Charity Societies and the ....'

'Stop!' Elizabeth said. 'Stop! I've done absolutely nothing without help. The Quaker ladies have been right behind me all the time, and my family have supported me, and countless other people too. Take Newgate, for example. Without the Governor's help we could have done nothing at all.'

'But it was all your idea,' her friend insisted.

Elizabeth Fry sighed wearily. 'When I was a young woman I was told that God had a special work for me. He wanted me to be a light to the blind, speech to the dumb and feet to the lame. That's all I've tried to do. And the amazing thing about working for the Lord is that he gives enough of his strength for each day's work. I've failed him often but he has never let me down.'

In 1845, when she was 65 years old, Elizabeth's strength failed and she died peacefully. Although she found it hard to accept praise on earth, when she died the

Lord had something to say to her. 'Well done, good and faithful servant. Welcome home.'

FACT FILE
Transportation: In the 1700s a prisoner could be sentenced to transportation for crimes such as stealing an apron or a side of bacon. Transportation meant being sent on a ship to either the American colonies or Botany Bay in Australia. They could be sentenced to 14 years in prison for stealing potatoes or a pair of shoes. Prior to Elizabeth Fry's involvement in prison reform on arrival at the colonies there was no accommodation or employment for the women.

Keynote: Elizabeth was someone who was anxious to lead a useful life. Opening a school, running a soup kitchen and tending the sick were not easy to do and then she also visited the prisons! We can learn from Elizabeth's life and determination. Elizabeth wanted to make her life useful to God - so should we.

Think: Elizabeth didn't concentrate on what she couldn't do. She saw a need and did her utmost to meet it. She was fearless and in God's strength accomplished much. Elizabeth must have been exhausted some days with all the work she did. She wasn't afraid to make a sacrifice. Jesus has done so much for us we will never be able to thank him enough. He has given his life and has given us salvation.

Prayer: Lord Jesus, I sometimes feel that I'm not able to do much, but show me what I can do and make me willing to do everything I can for you. Amen.

Amy Carmichael

For over a hundred years the flour mill in the seaside village of Millisle in Northern Ireland was where many of the villagers worked. Others farmed and fished, but they too were involved with the flour mill because the farmers took their grain there to be made into flour, and the fishermen's wives bought their bread flour at the mill. For all of that time the mill belonged to the Carmichael family.

1867 was an exciting year for the young Carmichael couple because they were expecting their first child. She was born just nine days before Christmas, and they called the little girl Amy Beatrice.

Amy was not to be the only child of the mill owners; six others were born over the years that followed.

It was a very busy household. There were probably only three times in the day when the house was quiet. One was when the children were all tucked up in bed and asleep and the other two were when the family met round the table to have morning and evening prayers.

Amy had a special time each night. 'After the nursery light was turned low and I was quite alone,' she told a friend once, 'I used to smooth a little place on the sheet and say aloud, but softly, to our Father, "Please come and sit with me".'

But Amy was not talking about her dad when she said that, she was talking about her heavenly Father. From when she was quite a little girl, Amy Carmichael loved God in a special way. He really was her very best friend and the person she most enjoyed spending time with.

'Would you like to come to Belfast with me?' Mrs Carmichael asked Amy one day.

Her face lit up. 'Yes please, I'd love to.'

Amy's younger brothers and sisters were full of questions.

'What are you going to Belfast for?'

'Can you bring back a treat for us?'

'What will you do when you're there?'

Mrs Carmichael laughed.

'We're going to Belfast to visit the shops,' she told one child. 'We will bring you back a treat,' she said to another. 'And one thing we're planning to do is go out for tea at a tea-shop.'

Amy felt so grown up at the thought of going to a tea-shop with her mother!

'Will you tell us all about it?' her youngest sister asked.

'Of course I will,' laughed Amy. 'I'll even tell you what I eat in the tea-shop!'

After a busy and exciting day in town, Amy sat down by the fire to tell the family all about her trip. They were especially interested in the tea-shop and in the pink icing on the biscuit Amy had with her sweet milky tea.

'A little girl came and stood near the door and looked though the window of the tea-shop,' she told the other children. 'Delicious cakes and sweets were set out in the window. As we left we saw the little girl with her face pressed close to the glass. She was looking at all the cakes and sweets. She was a poor little girl in a thin ragged dress. It was raining, and her bare feet on the wet pavement looked very cold.'

When Father called the family to have worship, Amy was not the only one who prayed for that poor little girl. And when her brothers and sisters were tucked up in bed that night, Amy sat on by the nursery fire. She couldn't get that poor girl out of her mind, so much so that she wrote a poem about her.

When I grow up and money have,
I know what I will do,
I'll build a great big lovely place
For little girls like you.

Years later, when Amy was grown-up, she thought about that little girl. Again she was in Belfast but this time she had not come from Millisle, she was going there. As she sat in the pony-pulled trap, warm in her rug, she saw a woman about her own age, ragged and with only sacking tied round her feet for shoes. Beside her were two little children, aged about eight and ten, and they reminded Amy of the tea-shop, of the biscuit with its pink icing, and of the poor little girl with her face pressed up against the glass as she looked at the cakes inside. Amy felt sad, especially because she was ill and exhausted herself.

'It's all so confusing,' she told her parents that evening as they finished their meal. 'I'm absolutely convinced that the Lord wants me to be a missionary overseas, yet first of all China Inland Mission turns me down, then, when I go out to work in Japan I'm so ill that I'm sent all the way home to recover.'

'Perhaps he wants you to serve him here,' her father suggested. 'There's plenty of need.'

Amy thought of the woman and her two little children and knew that was true.

'These are big issues to be discussing when you've just come halfway across the world,' her sensible mother said. 'There will be plenty of time to think it all through. In the meantime, you've to rest and concentrate on getting better.'

As Amy's eyes were already closing, she didn't need persuading to go to bed.

In 1895, when she had recovered her health, Amy was totally convinced that God wanted her in India.

Her family may have wondered about the wisdom of her decision but, as she was persuaded that was what the Lord was telling her to do, they waved their goodbyes and prayed for her daily. It was to the south of India that Amy went, to an area called Tinnevelly.

Much that Amy Carmichael saw in India was very beautiful. She loved the people, especially the dark-eyed children. She delighted in the colourfulness of clothes, in the beauty of the country, in the bustle of the market and in the friendship of the Christians she met there.

But there were other things, horrible things, that she could hardly believe were true. And the worst of these was to do with the Hindu temples.

'I can't take in what you're saying,' she told a converted Hindu woman. 'Tell me again to make sure I'm understanding you properly.'

'Amma,' the woman said, (that's Indian for Mother), 'what I am telling you is true. In this country a girl child is not a happy thing. Before a baby is born many Hindu parents tell the gods that if it is a girl they can have her as an offering. You see,' she went on, 'otherwise they will have to keep her, feed her and clothe her when what they really want to do is get rid of her and have another child, a boy.'

'Do you mean that they are killed as offerings?' the horrified missionary asked.

'No,' was the slow reply, 'they are not killed. But what happens is almost as bad. They are given to women who are prisoners in the temples and they are kept there and become prisoners too. Then, when they are five or six years old, they are given to the priests and are slaves to them until they are no longer young and beautiful.'

Amy gasped. 'What happens then?' she asked.

'They are put out of the temple,' the woman explained, 'and nobody wants to know them. It is as though they have a disease.'

'Where are they all now?'

'They are the devadassis, the little huddles of women you see in the poorest parts of the town.'

'But why are there not more of them?' Amy asked, thinking of all the little girls imprisoned within the temple walls.

Her friend looked sad. 'Many little girls in there,' she nodded towards the temple, 'don't live to get out.'

A shudder went down Amy's spine at the thought of what was happening just a short distance away. 'I must do something for those children,' she thought. 'I MUST do something.'

Soon afterwards, a baby girl was brought to her, tiny, fragile and creamy coloured, like a doll made of wax. Then two other tiny babies arrived. Amma was well named as she became the children's mother.

More babies followed. Toddlers were brought to her too, especially very pretty little girls whose parents thought that the gods would make them rich if they gave their daughters to them. Some temple women, who desperately didn't want girls to go through all they had been through, risked their lives to get new babies and toddlers out of the temple and into Amy's safe hands.

Lala was one of Amy's rescued children. When she was five, she was kidnapped from Dohnavur, which was where Amy's ever increasing family lived, and taken back to a temple in the mountains. Poor little Lala became ill and died. Amy was so sad when she heard that news but along with the news came an interesting story.

'I was there when Lala died,' a woman told her. 'She said things before she died that I remember and can tell you.'

'What did she say?' asked Amy.

'Lala said she was a Jesus child,' the woman said. 'And she did not seem afraid of dying. Then she said she saw three shining ones come into the room where she was lying. Her face was not fearful and when she saw the shining ones, Lala smiled. Then she died.'

For years Amy was mother to unwanted little girls. She gave them a home, she loved them as though they were her own and she taught them about the Lord Jesus. Not all of them survived because of the illnesses for which there were no medicines at that time, but Amy prayed that if any were to die they would, like Lala, die believing in Jesus.

One day Amy had an accident. She fell, breaking her leg and damaging her ankle badly. Nowadays she would probably have had surgery and would have been able to walk again. But things were different then, especially in a poor land like India.

For the twenty years and more that followed, Amy Carmichael was mostly in her bed and rarely out of her bedroom. That didn't stop her loving her rescued children and it gave her time to pray for them. It was as though she was a little girl again, lying on her bed asking Jesus to come and sit by her and let her talk to him about her rescued girls.

Amy also wrote poems and books as she rested in bed, many of which are still read now, many years after her death in 1951.

But one of Amy's poems was written about a time much earlier in her life. As a little brown eyed Irish girl, she prayed that God would make her eyes blue. She longed to have clear blue eyes.

'So she prayed for two blue eyes,
Said 'Goodnight',
Went to sleep in deep content
And delight.
Woke up early, climbed a chair
By a mirror. Where, O where
Could the blue eyes be? Not there;
Jesus hadn't answered.

Hadn't answered her at all;
Never more
Could she pray; her eyes were brown
As before.
Did a little soft wind blow?
Came a whisper soft and low,
'Jesus answered. He said, No;
Isn't No an answer?'

Jesus' answer to Amy's prayer for blue eyes was 'No'. Years later she understood why, for everyone in India has brown eyes, and she would not have fitted in at all if her eyes had been blue. God had work for Amy to do in India and he was preparing her to do it even when he chose the colour of her eyes.

FACT FILE
Eyes - when she was young, Amy spent a lot of time wishing her eyes were blue.

Look at your eyes in a mirror. The front of your eye contains the iris and the pupil - the circle of colour and the black dot in its centre - and it is their job to let light into the eye.

The pupil lets the light in and the iris decides the amount let in by controlling the size of pupil . The iris and the pupil together are just like a camera shutter that opens and closes.

Keynote: Amy had several setbacks before she got to India. First of all, she wasn't accepted by a missionary organisation and then she became ill. Later, Amy was confined to bed for almost twenty years.

But Amy trusted God and nothing stopped her from sharing the message of Jesus and caring for the many homeless children who came her way.

Learn from Amy's absolute trust in God in every situation.

 Think: Remember that God has made you just the way you are. Even the minute details were planned by him!

God cares about all the details of your life too. So don't be afraid to share your worries with him.

 Prayer: Lord Jesus, thank you for caring so much that you came to die for me. I'm sorry for the times that I complain about what I don't have. Help me to be thankful for everything you have given me. Amen.

Gladys Aylward

'I'm too old to go to Sunday School,' fourteen-year-old Gladys told her mother. 'Sunday School is for babies!'

Mrs Aylward looked sad. Her daughter was going through the terrible teens and she was getting rather tired of it.

'Well I hope you don't forget what you learned there,' her mother said, 'because if you do you'll come to a bad end.'

Gladys hardly heard what was said, she was too busy admiring herself in the mirror. Taking a comb, she redid her centre parting and smoothed out her dark hair on either side of it. 'I'm grown up now and I'm going to enjoy myself,' she decided.

Gladys wheezed as she breathed in cigarette smoke that night. She tried hard not to splutter. What would her friends think of her if she did that.

'Is this your first smoke?' a fair-haired girl asked her.

Still trying not to go into a fit of coughing, Gladys shook her head.

'No,' she lied eventually, 'I've smoked in secret for ages.'

Her friends didn't believe a word she said.

Trying to look as though she did this every day, Gladys put the cigarette to her mouth again. Although by then her stomach was heaving, she smoked her way to the bitter end of her first cigarette and reckoned she'd grown up.

As soon as she stopped Sunday School, Gladys filed everything to do with Christianity away in the back of her mind. She thought it was just for babies and grannies.

She found a job as a housemaid in the centre of London and her free time was spent with her various boyfriends, sometimes gambling, sometimes drinking and always smoking.

For the next twelve years she didn't give God a thought, even though she used his name as a swear word. But God hadn't forgotten Gladys.

'Where are you going tonight?' she asked a group of her friends one afternoon.

They looked embarrassed. 'We're going to a meeting in Kensington.'

'What kind of a meeting?'

'A religious one.'

'Can I come?' Gladys asked.

Her friends looked at each other.

Gladys grinned. 'Anything for a laugh,' she said.

But that night things changed for Gladys Aylward. She heard things she'd forgotten from Sunday School days - that Jesus loved her, that Jesus died for her and that he wanted to forgive all her sins. The past twelve years spun round in her head and Gladys realised she had done many wrong things. Before she left that meeting she asked Jesus to forgive all her sins and to be her Saviour and friend.

Instead of going drinking on her next night off, Gladys went to a Young Life Campaign meeting and she went every week from then on. That was where she picked up a magazine which said that missionaries were needed in China.

Gladys applied to go as a missionary but had to leave college after three months because she'd learned almost nothing at all. Everything she heard and read seemed to go out of her head as soon as it went in. For a while she looked after two retired lady missionaries, then she worked in Swansea as a missionary to needy women there. She walked along the docks looking for them, then took them back to the mission hall.

China was never far from Gladys's mind, though, and she was quite sure that God wanted her to go there. One day, as she read in her Bible that when Nehemiah felt God wanted him in Jerusalem he went there, she suddenly thought to herself, 'If God wants me in China then I'll have to save up and go.' She had just moved to a new job and had been given 15p for her travelling expenses. Looking at the three coins, she thought, 'it's not much but it's a start.'

Because Gladys took every job she could fit into her spare time she had soon saved up £3.

'How much is a ticket to China?' she asked in a travel shop.

'China!' the man said.

Gladys pulled herself up to her full height. 'Yes,' she agreed. 'China.'

'Come back in two days and I'll tell you,' the booking clerk said.

Two days later, Gladys was back.

'If you were to go by train through Europe, Russian and Siberia it would cost £47.50,' she was told.

Putting her £3 on the desk she explained that was all she had, but that she'd come in every time she'd saved £1 and pay it up £1 at a time.

The man scratched his head in wonder as his strangest ever customer closed the door behind her.

Before she had saved all she needed, Gladys heard about Mrs Lawson, an elderly missionary in China, who was looking for a companion. A letter was written right away and, after what seemed like ages, Gladys had a reply. Mrs Lawson wanted her to come to China!

On 15th October 1932, just after she was 30, Gladys Aylward set off by train for China. Her luggage consisted of two suitcases, one of them full of food for the journey, a bedroll, a small stove, a kettle and a saucepan. She looked like a one-woman Girl Guide camp!

The journey to China was full of adventures, not all of them nice. In Russia officials tried to force her to stay because they wanted her to work in a factory. That was because they read 'missionary' on her passport and thought that it said 'machinery'! Later she found herself in the middle of a war and one night Gladys slept outside with the sound of wolves howling in the distance. Her fresh food grew stale and in Siberia it was so cold that her tinned food froze solid. Nearly a month after leaving London, on 10th November, Gladys Aylward took her first steps on Chinese soil. Very soon she met up with Mrs Lawson and discovered what her job would involve.

'I'm going to open an inn for muleteers,' the elderly lady explained. 'And when they stay for the night we'll tell them about Jesus.'

Gladys was startled. 'But I don't speak any Chinese,' she said.

Mrs Lawson laughed. 'Neither do the mules. Your job will be to stand outside the inn and grab the mules by their manes as they pass by. By evening the muleteers will be so tired they won't argue about coming here for the night. For the time being you'll have to let Mr Lu, the evangelist, do the talking. And when he's not here, I'll do it myself.'

Having come from London, Gladys was more than a little worried about the mules.

'Do they bite?' she asked.

Shaking her head, Mrs Lawson said that they were fine if caught in the right way!

Gladys was not reassured.

Before long the new missionary knew exactly which part of the mule to grab and most nights she had hauled so many inside that the inn was full. It became a popular place for muleteers to stay. Not only did they get shelter for the night, they were told stories by a white woman too.

Mrs Lawson fell ill the year after Gladys went out and, when she died, Gladys was left to run the inn with Mr Lu's help. By then she had learned enough Chinese to do some of the speaking and she felt, at last, that she was a real missionary in China.

At that time Japan and China were at war and even the inn was bombed. It became a very dangerous part of the world to be in. Refugees moved from place to place depending on where the fighting was but Gladys stayed where she was. Everybody knew her because she was the only European in that part of China.

'We can't take Dusty Heap with us,' a group of guerrillas said, as they thrust a boy into her home one day. 'You look after him.'

Gladys looked at the lad. 'His name suits him,' she thought, 'he's so ragged and dirty.'

Suddenly it was as if a magnet drew children to her and before long she was running a home for over a hundred homeless children!

The war crept closer. 'What are we to do with the children?' she asked Mr Lu.

It was agreed that she would stay where she was and he would take the children to safety.

'I'll be back in a month,' he said. 'Pray for us as we go.'

Day by day Gladys prayed for Mr Lu and for the children, that they would get out of the war zone to a safe place.

By the time the month had passed, the missionary found herself looking after another hundred children. 'Where are they all coming from?' she often asked herself. And where is Mr Lu?

'You must take these children and leave here,' a Chinese Army officer told her.

Gladys shook her head. 'God called me here and I'll stay here. But please take the children to somewhere safe.'

The officer ordered his men to escort the children to Chong Tsuen, a town a short distance away.

Only when he came back to her door with a Japanese poster saying that she was a wanted person, did Gladys agree to leave and when she did she had to duck bullets and dodge soldiers for the first part of the way. At Chong Tsuen Gladys was reunited with the children. But even there it was not safe so she decided to take them to Shensi. Like the Pied Piper of Hamlyn she set out through the countryside with a hundred children in a long trail behind her. She carried the little ones in turns and the older children did the same. At Shensi the missionary discovered that Mr Lu was in prison. No wonder he hadn't come home.

But even Shensi wasn't a safe place for them. How Gladys must have prayed before taking a hundred children over mountains thousands of feet high to reach the safety of Sian. For twelve days they walked, begging in little villages for food and sleeping in whatever shelter they could find.

'Let's sing a song,' she shouted, when exhausted children thought they could walk

not one step more. And when they tired of
singing, she played games with them. 'I spy,
with my little eye, something that starts
with b.' 'Boys!' one child called out. Gladys
shook her head. 'Birds!' called another. And
when they were bored and tired of that
little game, the missionary had to think of
something else.

For twelve days they snaked through
the mountains, for twelve nights they slept
cuddled together for warmth.

'How far is it now?' children pleaded,
hundreds of times a day.

'Every step is one step nearer,' Gladys
said, to encourage them on.

'What's that down there?' a boy asked,
when even the missionary thought she could
go no further.

'It's the Yellow River!' someone shouted.
We're nearly there!

A cheer went through the crowd of
children, and excitement gave them the
energy to go on. But, relieved though she
was to see the river, Gladys knew that wasn't
the end of their journey. There was still a
long way to go.

God knew that the weary travellers
weren't able to take much more. They
crossed the river in boats then, after a

further two days' walking, they were able to travel, for most of what was left of the journey, hidden among the coal on a train. When Gladys eventually delivered her children to the safety of an orphanage near Sian, she collapsed, ill and utterly exhausted. The villagers who found her expected her to die. It was a long time until Gladys Aylward was fit to travel and her next journey was home to England for a much needed rest, before going back to her beloved China.

FACT FILE

Aeroplanes - Gladys Aylward travelled all the way to China by train and it took her almost a month. How much easier it would have been for her to fly there, as we can do today!

The story of air travel began just a year after Gladys was born. The first true aeroplane was Flyer 1, piloted by an American engineer called Orville Wright on 17th December 1903.

Within 16 years an aeroplane had flown across the Atlantic Ocean and air travel has gone on developing rapidly ever since.

Keynote: If, when she was young, Gladys had been told that one day she would lead over 100 children on a 12 day trek across a mountain range in China she would probably have thought it was impossible. But she soon learnt that with God, nothing is impossible.

Learn, as Gladys did, that God can make even the impossible happen!

Think: Gladys didn't just say that she trusted God, she proved that God is worth trusting in everything she did.

Think of a challenge or a problem you're facing right now. Remember that God is on your side and you can trust him to help you through it!

Prayer: Lord Jesus, sometimes I worry about things and when I face a problem I panic. Help me to trust in you completely no matter what and to go ahead knowing that you are with me. Amen.

Mary Slessor

Mary crawled under the loom, found the two broken ends of jute, tied them together and then crawled out again. Her hair was tied up in a cloth to prevent it getting caught in the workings of the loom. Some workers in the factory had had great chunks of hair yanked out of their scalps by being careless and Mary didn't want that to happen to her. Mary had lovely, golden red hair and a temper to match it.

Clambering back to her place in front of the loom Mary Slessor watched the machine carefully. If the boss saw her taking her eyes off it there would be a clip on the ear or worse.

The clatter of machinery ripped through Mary Slessor's head. To get away from it she imagined the seashore at Aberdeen on a stormy day, imagined that the noise was the roar of the waves and that she could feel the salt spray on her face. But if she thought too much about Aberdeen the only salt she felt was salt tears.

'I wish we hadn't had to come to Dundee,' the girl said aloud. It didn't matter if she spoke out loud in the factory, as nobody could hear a word that was said. 'I wish Dad hadn't drunk so much that he lost his job.' Mary's life was a difficult one. Her family was poor. Some of Mary's brothers and sisters had died. They didn't have enough money to pay for a doctor. Then Mary's father drank too much and made the whole family's life a misery. Mary often went to bed hungry and right now she was ravenous.

She couldn't hear it but she felt her stomach rumbling. 'I wish I didn't always feel so hungry.' Just then the jute snapped. Mary pulled the cloth over her hair and ducked under the machine again.

They always did it, the Slessor children, they listened at the door before they went in to hear if their dad was raging. What they wanted to hear was him snoring because if he fell into a drunken sleep he wouldn't cause trouble for a few hours. Mary listened, sounds of snoring reassured her and she went inside.

'Well, Mary,' her mother said. 'That's another week over.'

'Thank goodness for that,' the thirteen-year-old sighed. 'I just live for Saturday evenings and the great feeling that I don't need to go back to work till Monday.'

Mrs Slessor put her arm round her daughter's shoulder. 'I'm really sorry you have to work,' she said. 'But you and I need to earn enough to keep the family fed. Since your brother died your dad's not been fit for anything.'

'Is that really what made him like this?' Mary nodded towards her drunk father.

'Yes it is,' her mother said. 'And try to remember that when you feel angry with him.'

'It's Sunday,' Mary's little sister said, shaking her awake. 'And the sun's shining.'

Mary Slessor rubbed her eyes. She didn't want to miss a minute of Sunday or a minute of sunshine. All week she went to the mill in the dark and came home in the dark.

'You get dressed and we'll go for a walk before church.'

The girls pulled on their clothes. On the way through the back court they splashed cold water on their faces. Then, hand in hand, they walked along the road, through the town to the River Tay.

'Look how it sparkles,' the little girl said. 'It's like a treasure chest.'

'It sparkles just like your eyes,' Mary told her sister as she tousled her hair. 'Would you like a piggyback home?'

'I knew you'd be here on time,' Mrs Slessor said, as they went in the door. 'We're just about ready.'

The family, apart from Mr Slessor, walked to church and settled in the pew to enjoy the service. Their home was dark and dingy, but the church was bright and clean. The week was hard work, but in church they could relax. But most of all, and best of all, they wanted to hear about Jesus' love. Mary's mother was in love with the Lord and the warmth of her faith made her children long to be the same.

'Sunday School time!' said the littlest Slessor. 'I love the stories.'

Mary did too, especially the stories about missionaries in Africa.

Back in the mill on Monday, Mary thought about Africa. She thought about all the little African children who had never heard about Jesus and she wished she was with them.

'I'd love to be there with all the little African children round me, playing games with them and telling them Bible stories... but I don't think that will ever happen... I'll probably never go past the edge of Dundee!'

Mary thought that her dreams would never amount to anything and that nothing would ever happen. But when she was twenty-eight years old her dreams came true. She sailed for Calabar in Africa (south eastern Nigeria today) on the SS Ethiopa!

'I think I can see land.' she said, five weeks after leaving Liverpool.

'That's Calabar,' her fellow passenger told her.

Mary's heart raced. She could hardly speak for excitement.

'Look at the children!' she squealed, as they neared the harbour. 'Look at their bright eyes! Look at their shiny white teeth! Look at their beautiful curly hair!'

The missionary who met Mary could hardly get the young woman away from the little group of children who surrounded her as soon as she got off the ship. Eventually she forced herself to wave goodbye to them and go with her new colleague to the mission house.

'Tell me all about Calabar,' Mary pleaded, as she ate a meal with the missionaries she was staying with.

'You begin,' said the wife.

Her husband finished what was on his plate before speaking.

'Most of the people here don't know anything about Jesus. A lot of them believe in evil spirits and are scared stiff of them. The villages are run by chiefs and what the chief says goes. Anyone who goes against the chief doesn't last long.'

'Eat up your meal,' the missionary's wife encouraged.

Mary had been so interested in what she was hearing that she'd forgotten to eat!

'The women have a bad time,' the wife went on. 'They're just slaves to the men and some terrible things happen to them.'

'What kind of things?' Mary asked.

'I think we've talked enough about the sad side of Calabar for now,' her husband said. 'Would you like a short walk?'

No sooner were they outside than a group of children gathered round Mary.

'I think it's your red hair they're interested in,' her companion said.

Mary knelt down, picked up two stones, threw one in the air then hit it with the other. The children watched. She did it again, then a third time. Suddenly there was a scramble of children trying to find two stones. Mary smiled when the missionaries went back into their house in case they were hit by flying stones.

'Despite the awful stories,' she thought, 'I'm going to love it here.'

After a time with the missionary couple, Mary moved a little way into the country. By then she knew some of the language.

'I heard that baby crying in the bush,' an African woman said to two others as they passed Mary Slessor one afternoon.

'It's amazing it's still alive. It's been out there for five days now.'

'What are you talking about?' Mary asked the women.

They shrugged their shoulders.

'Tell me what you were saying,' she insisted.

The story she heard sent a shiver down her spine.

'One of the village women had a baby five days ago,' she was told. 'The mother died, so the baby was put out in the bush to die too.'

Mary could hardly believe her ears.

'It had an evil spirit,' the woman went on. 'That's why its mother died and that's why nobody else wants it. If anyone took the baby they would die too.'

Mary was on her feet.

'Where is it?' she demanded. 'Where did the cries come from?'

Two women shook their heads. The third pointed vaguely into the bush.

'Tell me exactly where you heard it, exactly!'

Mary listened to the directions and ran like the wind. When she thought she'd gone far enough, she stopped and listened. But her breathing was so noisy that she had to wait for a minute before she heard a cry. Then she followed the sound, till she came to a tiny baby girl lying under a dried-up bush.

'My lamb,' she said, lifting the baby into her arms. 'My lamb.'

Nobody went near her when she went back to the village. The Calabar people believed that Mary would be punished by the evil spirits. They were scared and didn't want to go anywhere near her just in case something awful happened to them. They didn't know any better and when they caught sight of her they would say, 'Just you wait and see. The evil spirit will kill her.'

Mary overheard these comments but ignored them all. Holding the little baby girl gently but firmly in her arms, she bathed the tiny body and put the only cream she had on her skin. The little girl had been terribly eaten by white ants.

Mary really didn't think the little girl would live. But then she thought what a strong baby she must have been to survive the first five days of her life in the bush with no milk at all.

But the people were still suspicious.'The white woman with red hair will die soon,' women said to each other, as Mary cared for the baby. They stayed away from the missionary and the little one. In their opinion she was dangerous.

But Mary Slessor didn't die, and eventually the villagers decided that the baby didn't have an evil spirit at all. Perhaps, after all, they could keep babies whose mothers died.

One day there was a great sadness is Mary's village.

'What's wrong?' she asked the women.

'My sister has had twins,' a sad faced African woman said, 'so the babies will be killed and she'll be chased away into the bush.'

'WHAT!!!' roared Mary, jumping to her feet. 'Take me to her!'

The poor woman hesitated.

'NOW!'

There was a huddle of people around the hut. As long as she was there, Mary knew the babies were safe.

'Explain what's happening,' she pleaded.

'When twin babies are born one of them is the child of an evil spirit. But, as we don't know which one, they're both killed. And because the mother has had a spirit child, she's put out in the bush to be killed by wild animals.'

'NO SHE IS NOT!'

There was no arguing with Mary Slessor.

'I'll look after the twins,' she said. 'Just wait and see what happens. Neither of them is the child of an evil spirit. The Lord God made them both.'

Because of Mary's anger and determination, the woman survived and so did the children. Mary was gathering quite a little family about her. The villagers were impressed that there didn't seem to be evil spirits in the babies. News about that spread and eventually the people of Calabar stopped leaving babies whose mothers died out in the bush and they stopped killing twins.

'Jesus loves children,' Mary told her adopted family. 'He loves them so much that he came down from heaven for them.'

Village women, and even some men, sat where they could hear her speaking.

'Does your Jesus love us too?' the women asked later.

Mary told them the Bible story and some of the people believed it.

When Mary Slessor went to Calabar the people she met believed in evil spirits and that led to much fear and unhappiness. But when they trusted in the Lord Jesus their fear and unhappiness was taken away and she could see the difference in their sparkling eyes.

FACT FILE
Africa - another famous Scot who went to Africa was David Livingstone, who is regarded as the greatest of Africa's explorers. Very little was known about the continent of Africa before Livingstone came along!

On one expedition on the Zambesi river, Livingstone discovered some amazing waterfalls. He called them the 'Victoria Falls' after Queen Victoria, but they were already known as 'the smoke that thundered' by the African people who lived nearby. Why not look up an atlas and try to find them?

Keynote: Mary was never slow to speak up when she saw evil around her but she didn't just point out the sins. She showed people an alternative and better way. She showed them what Jesus wanted them to do. Learn from Mary's eagerness to tell others what Jesus wants us to do.

Think: As a child Mary had a very strong character and a short temper, but God went on to use her determination and strong will in a wonderful way.

You are unique and God can use you in a special way too. Start by doing small things for him and don't be shy to tell others about Jesus. He's worth sharing!

Prayer: Lord Jesus, thank you for making me just the way I am. Please show me what I can do for you and give me the courage to speak up for you whenever I can. Amen.

Catherine Booth

The little girl sat in front of the fire with her picture book. Martha, her doll, was at her side. 'See Martha,' she said, pointing to the words in the book. 'Those letters are c-a-t and the word says cat.' She turned the page. 'Those letters are f-o-x and the word says fox.' She pointed to the x. 'But that sometimes means kiss,' she explained then picked up her doll and kissed her.

'She really is a clever little girl,' smiled Mrs Mumford's visitor. 'What age did you say she is?'

'Catherine is three,' she replied. 'She just seems to pick up letters as I read books to her.'

'You'll have to watch you don't exhaust her brain,' warned the visitor.

Mrs Mumford smiled. She knew that Catherine's brain was not very likely to tire out.

By the time the girl was five, in 1834, she had regular lessons from her mother although she didn't go to school. The book they read most together was the Bible and by Catherine's twelfth birthday she had read it right through eight times! But life was not all work. When her father went on business trips some distance away from their home in Boston in Lincolnshire, he sometimes took her with him.

'Would you like to learn to drive the horse?' Father asked, when she was about nine years old.

Catherine's eyes shone. 'Yes please, Papa.'

Pulling her on to his knee, he handed her the reins, while holding them gently to stop the horse should he bolt. 'Easy now,' he said. 'Just let the horse have his head.' The creature walked along quite steadily. 'Now let's try more difficult things,' suggested Father, at a quiet part of the road. 'Pull the right rein gently and see what happens. The horse turned towards the right and walked on. 'Now do the same with the left rein.' The girl did as she was told and was delighted when the horse immediately obeyed her instruction and turned towards the left.

'Mama!' she called out, when they returned home that afternoon, 'I can drive the horse and carriage! Papa let me drive!'

'Catherine has a way with horses,' her father said.

Mrs Mumford looked at her daughter. 'You love all animals, don't you?'

It was because Catherine loved animals that she was brokenhearted when her dog was put down when she was twelve. She found it difficult to talk about how upset she was, though she did pray about it. Soon after this sad happening, the girl went to school. And how she loved it! But that freedom didn't last for long. Catherine developed a problem with her spine and had to lie in bed for a whole year.

'What would you like to do today?' her mother asked every morning when they had finished their lessons. But she already knew the answer.

'I'm quite happy with my books,' was the girl's daily reply.

For a year Catherine read books that most adults don't even read. At the end of it, when her back was better, she had read very thick and serious books about God. For the next few years she puzzled about the Lord. Did he really love her? Did she need to be forgiven? How could she know she would go to heaven? But, when she was seventeen, the truth dawned on her. Jesus did love her. Yes, she did need to be forgiven. And yes, she knew she was going to heaven because that's what the Bible said happened to those who trusted in Jesus. And she was convinced that the Bible was true. Catherine was happy at last!

Catherine and her mother were at a Christian meeting three years later and it was there that they first met William Booth, an apprentice pawnbroker. However, by the time he and Catherine fell in love, William was on his way to becoming a travelling preacher. For six years the young couple wrote to each other, first once a week, then twice a week, then nearly every day until they were married on July 16th, 1855. They were both 26 years old.

'How are you managing all the travelling?' Mrs Mumford asked Catherine in a letter.

Her daughter answered the next day. 'Dear Mama, William's tours are not as exhausting as you would think. We are usually in each place for about a month and people make us feel very much at home everywhere we go. I've seen some interesting places I'd never visited before. Hull was full of fishwives. They travel round the coast depending on where the herring is being landed. Then we were in Sheffield where cutlery is made. After that we were a month in Halifax. Please don't worry about the travelling, Mama. William looks after me wonderfully well.'

'I've been asked to be Superintendent in Gateshead,' William told his wife some years later.

She thought for a moment. 'It would be nice to stay in one place though I've loved our time of travelling.'

William's preaching still sometimes took him away from home, but Catherine was busy about her own things. By then she had begun to do Christian work herself. This started when she spoke to women on the street about the Lord Jesus and before long she was taking services!

'I'm very surprised at myself.' she told William, when he returned from two weeks away.

He wondered what was coming.

'The Lord seemed to be leading me to speak to some people who where drunk. At first I felt very nervous. But he gave me the words to say and now I find I can approach such people and tell them about the Lord Jesus.'

William was not as surprised as Catherine had been. He had watched her becoming more involved in the work even though she now had their children to look after. 'Where would this lead?' he wondered.

From Gateshead they moved south, eventually to London. More and more invitations came for Catherine to speak and fewer came for William. It was a difficult time for them. One night she was home before him and sitting by the fire when he came in.

'Oh Catherine,' he said, slumping down in his chair, 'when I passed the drinking dens tonight, I seemed to hear a voice in my head asking me where else I could find so many men in need of the good news about Jesus as in places like that. I feel that the Lord is leading me into working here in the East End of London with these men and women.'

Catherine gazed into the fire. 'Where will the money come to support us?' she wondered. 'The men in the drinking dens certainly won't keep seven of us in food and clothes and there's another baby on the way.'

But when she spoke, that was not what she said. 'The Lord has never let us down before. If he wants you to do that, he'll provide for us.'

William wrote to a Christian newspaper, outlining his plans. 'Because most people in areas like this don't go to church we will visit them and hold services where they are, in the open air, in theatres and other places too. We'll go where people are, not wait for them to come to us.' And that was the very beginning of The Salvation Army.

It was 1870 and, after a huge effort to raise money, the People's Mission Hall was opened in one of the poorest parts of London.

'When are your meetings?' a visitor at the opening service, asked Catherine.

'We're open every night,' was the surprising reply. 'There will always be an open door here for people in need. That's why we have a soup kitchen. Have you any idea how many hungry people there are around here?'

The visitor took some pound notes out of his wallet and gave them to Catherine.

'Here,' he said. 'That will buy vegetables for tomorrow's soup.'

The Salvation Army reached out to the poor and needy, taking the good news about Jesus in one hand and soup and warm clothes in the other. Where people were hungry, the Army was there to feed them. Where people were cold, the Army was there to give them clothes. And where people needed Jesus, the Salvation Army was there to tell them that he loved them enough to die for them. William became General Booth, a general in the Lord's army. And Catherine was given a title too, the Army Mother. The Booths never forgot their call to serve the people with a drink problem, treating them with a love that they found nowhere else. Men, women and young people were loved into the Salvation Army, loved by the General and the Army Mother, and loved by the Lord Jesus Christ.

'Tell me about a Salvation Army meeting,' a Scottish friend wrote to Catherine when he sent her money for the work.

'If you were in London,' she wrote back, 'you would know us right away because of our Army uniforms and flags. The men wear hats and the women wear bonnets with crimson bands on which are written The Salvation Army. Our meetings are lively, lots of singing and Hallelujahs. There is nothing dismal and dull about our services at all. People come in off the streets just because of our cheerful music and joyful singing. Most of our people are poor, and many of them would never go into an ordinary church. But everyone is welcome at the Army. Women and children have a special place. Women officers preach in the Army as well as men and we hold special services and missions for children.'

'Will you come and help us on the streets this evening?' Catherine asked a church visitor to their work.

'What would I have to do?' the young woman wanted to know.

'Two of you will patrol the streets you're given, looking out for people in need. You'll find wives whose husbands have thrown them out, sometimes wearing only nightclothes with a coat on top, and often with children too. You'll find young people who have argued with their parents and run away. And you'll find men and women who have mental health problems too.'

The woman looked horrified. 'But I've never met people like that before. I wouldn't know what to say.'

Catherine Booth looked into her eyes.

'How long have you been a Christian?'

'Eight years.'

'And you've never reached out to the people who need you most?' the Army Mother said sadly.

The young woman's expression softened. 'No,' she said. 'I've not. But I will tonight, and I will from now on.'

Later that evening the two women met again in the soup kitchen. The visitor was flushed with excitement.

'Did God use you tonight?' asked Catherine Booth.

Her companion nodded her head. 'He surely did and he taught me a lesson.'

'What was that?' the older woman wanted to know.

Smiling, the visitor put into words what one evening on the streets meant to her. 'I've discovered that being a Christian means being like Jesus, and tonight I've done what he did, I've held out my hand in love to people who aren't loveable but there's one thing I'd like to ask you.'

Catherine wondered what that would be.

'I know you have a big family,' she said. 'How did you manage to bring them up and still be so busy for the Lord. Didn't they feel neglected?'

The Army Mother smiled at the thought of her children. 'I've always made time for my children,' she answered. 'You see, they are the first mission field the Lord gave me. Every one of them is a Christian and all but one is a Salvation Army Officer.'

'Thank you, that answers my question. You're the Army Mother and you're a real mother to your own children too.'

FACT FILE
Railways - Catherine was born just the year before the first passenger carrying railway opened in England in 1830.

For hundreds of years the fastest way of getting from place to place over land was on horseback or horsedrawn carriage. Catherine and her father travelled like that.

Railways brought the biggest ever change in people's way of travelling and by the time Catherine was in her fifties, most of the major countries in the world had railway lines and more were being built every year.

Keynote: Catherine brought God's love to people who were unloved. She cared for the drunk, fed the hungry, clothed the homeless and told them about Jesus.

Learn from how Catherine loved the unloved and be prepared to roll up your sleeves and work hard for God!

Think: Look around you and see what you could do to show God's love in a practical way.

Why not donate some of your toys or clothes to a charity shop or do a sponsored activity to raise money for helping the homeless? You could have fun and help others at the same time!

Prayer: Lord Jesus, open my eyes to see that all around me there are people who need help and who need you. Show me what I can do to make a difference. Help me to say and do the right thing. Amen.

Jackie Pullinger

'This is like a huge xylophone!', Jackie told her twin, as she ran a toy along the radiator. She banged a little harder. A satisfying 'Bong!' went from that radiator along the pipes to the one in the kitchen. Mrs Pullinger ran out to see what was wrong with the central heating. She was met by twin grins.

'I'd rather you stuck to the piano,' she laughed.

Jackie's twin climbed on to the stool and tried to play a tune on the piano, not easy when you are just four years old. But Jackie sat down with her back to the radiator and had a long think. She knew she was always found out when she did something naughty and she tried to work out if it would be better to try to be good. These were complicated thoughts for a very little girl.

At Sunday School a year later, a missionary told the children about the work she did.

'Perhaps God wants you to go to the mission field,' the woman said.

Jackie thought about that. In her mind she saw a big green field, that's what she imagined a mission field would look like. In the middle of the field there was a mud hut and she tried hard to imagine herself sitting outside it. 'That's what it must be like to be on the mission field,' she decided. Then she thought a bit more about what the woman had said and decided that God wanted everyone to be on the mission field. The picture in her mind's eye must have looked a little crowded by then!

'You have a real gift for music,' Jackie's teacher said, when she had started boarding school. 'What was your first instrument?'

The girl thought. 'The radiator, Miss,' she answered truthfully.

Her teacher wondered if she had heard correctly. She had. 'Well, I think you should stick to the piano and oboe. We don't have musical radiators here.'

Jackie looked at the radiator under the window and wondered if what her teacher had said was true. But she did work hard at her piano and oboe, and after leaving school she went to the Royal College of Music in London to continue her studies there.

It was when she was a student that Jackie came to believe in God in a new way. She discovered that he was really interested in her, really loved her and that he really did want her to become a missionary.

'Dear Sir,' she wrote at the top of several identical letters, all going to different missionary societies, 'I'm convinced that God wants me to be a missionary. I have studied music and I'd like to know if I could go abroad with your organisation as a music teacher.'

One by one the answers came back.

'I'm afraid we don't need music teachers at present.'

'We cannot consider your application until you have some experience.'

'We do not take people under twenty-five years of age.'

Jackie placed all the answers on the table and frowned over them. 'So where do I go from here?' she asked herself. And she asked a minister friend the same question.

'If you really believe that's what God wants you to do, then go ahead and do it,' was his advice. 'Buy yourself a ticket for as far away as you can afford and get off where the Lord tells you to.'

That made perfect sense to Jackie Pullinger and that's how she came to be disembarking from a ship in Hong Kong in the mid-1960s.

Having spent nearly all her money on travel, Jackie needed to find a job as soon as she arrived in Hong Kong. Before long she was doing some music teaching, not full time, but enough to feed her and pay for accommodation. 'What do you want me to do here?' she asked her heavenly Father every day in her prayers.

'Will you come and visit my school in Hak Nam?' a Christian lady called Mrs Donnithorne asked her.

Jackie agreed to go. And it was on that visit she discovered the answer to her prayers.

'Hak Nam is the Chinese name for the Walled City,' her guide told her as they walked. 'It's the poorest and most notorious area of Hong Kong. When you're in Hak Nam you need eyes in the back of your head.'

Jackie followed her friend though a tiny gap between two shops into the Walled City. What hit her first was the smell, then the slime under her feet, then darkness because the buildings were crushed together with only a tiny space between them, then it was water. Or was it?

'You need eyes on the top of your head too,' Mrs Donnithorne said, ducking into the shelter of a doorway. 'Rubbish is just thrown out of windows into the alleys where people walk.'

Jackie wiped her hair then looked at her hand. It wasn't water, and from the colour and the smell of it she decided not to try to work out what it was.

A boy of about twelve bumped into Jackie as he made his unsteady way long the alley.

'Poor lad,' the teacher said. 'He came to my school once and now he doesn't even recognise me. He's pumped full of drugs and he always is.'

'And look at her,' the elderly lady pointed to a girl aged no more than eight. 'She does that about eighteen hours a day. If she falls asleep someone kicks her awake again and tells her to get on with it.'

Jackie's eyes took a minute to get used to the darkness in which the little girl sat.

She was pushing bright red plastic flower petals on to green wire stems. On one side of her was a mountain of petals bigger than herself and on the other was a pile of finished flowers. The little girl's fingers moved quickly but her eyes didn't move at all. They looked dull and dead as she stared straight ahead.

'Why isn't she at school?' Jackie asked.

The older lady explained. 'In some Chinese communities, and the Walled City is one of them, Chinese parents reckon that their children should repay all that they've cost their parents. That little girl is working to pay back what's been spent on her food and clothes since she was born.'

Jackie looked at the child and wondered what her parents were charging for the rags she was wearing.

Soon Jackie realised that the Walled City was where God wanted her to work.

When Mrs Donnithorne asked if she would teach in her school, Jackie's immediate answer was 'yes'. And on Sundays the new young missionary peddled at what seemed a hundred miles an hour to keep the harmonium going for the service that was held in the school.

'I think God wants me to start a youth club here,' Jackie told Mrs Donnithorne soon afterwards.

The elderly lady, whose heart was full of love for the people of Hak Nam, was thrilled. 'Is this the person God's sending to make a difference here?' she wondered.

The room was bare apart from an ancient table tennis table, a dart board on the wall, skittles, a few board games and a bookshelf of Christian books.

'What's going on here?' two boys demanded, as they forced their way in.

'I'm starting a youth club,' Jackie told them.

One sneered. 'What's in it for you?'

She shook her head. 'Nothing at all.'

'Whose gang's running it?' the other boy asked.

Everything in the Walled City was run by one or other of the famous Chinese Triad gangs.

'No gang,' Jackie told them.

'That'll be right,' growled the first boy, picking up a table tennis bat as he spoke.

Soon a game was underway and, as if by magnetism, other boys came in to referee the match.

'Thank you, Lord,' Jackie prayed that night. 'The youth club's up and running!'

But the work wasn't easy. Nobody in the Walled City trusted anyone else. Each Triad gang thought one of the other gangs was supporting the youth club. Drug addicts caused trouble, fights broke out, murders happened round about, and the only people there to keep any kind of peace were the Triad gangs. Regular police work wouldn't have lasted quarter-of-an-hour in Hak Nam.

When the police did try to crack down, they just arrested people then found crimes to charge them with. The better they knew someone's face, the more likely they were to arrest him even if they didn't have anything to charge him with. There were always plenty of crimes going spare.

Power ruled and the power changed depending on where in the Walled City you were and which was top gang at the time. But good things happened in that bad place.

A boy, who had more of a skeleton than a body, came to the youth club regularly. He was into gang wars and gambling and he took drugs too.

'Jesus loves you,' Jackie told him one evening.

He wouldn't look at her. 'Oh yeah,' he said, not believing that anyone at all could love him.

'When Jesus was on earth he spent time on the streets with people like you. He didn't sit around in churches waiting for good guys to turn up.'

The boy was interested.

Jackie told him about the Lord, that he loved bad people so much that he died to save them so that one day they could go to heaven.

There was a stifled sound beside her. When Jackie turned round, the boy was praying and crying, asking Jesus to forgive him. When he opened his eyes they were full of tears but they were beautiful. For the first time ever that boy was really happy.

After some years working in the Walled City, Jackie Pullinger wrote a letter to a friend from the Royal College of Music, telling her about the work she was doing.

'It started off as a youth club but it's grown from that. We now have four houses where people can stay. So many of them have just been kicked out of their homes. Some lived in drug dens anyway so they're better out of them.

We have girls who have had babies staying there too. Many of our guests have been drug addicts and have criminal records as long as my arm. A number of them have run away from cruel homes where terrible things were done to them. And we have some older people staying too. I didn't want that at first but it turned out to be a good idea.

Because I can't be in four places at once, I have helpers working with me. And before you write back to nag me, yes, I do still play my oboe! I wouldn't like to be without it.'

Maria was a young teenager when Jackie met her. She had been brought up in a terrible home and, when things became unbearable, she escaped from the Walled City and found work in another part of Hong Kong. Jackie didn't forget the girl and kept praying for her. One day they met again.

'I'm in terrible debt,' Maria confessed. 'I've been working in a ballroom. The man there gave me dresses to wear for my work and now he's making me pay for them. I'm his slave until I pay and I haven't got any money.' She began to cry.

'What about the money you earn?' Jackie asked.

'He won't give me anything till I've paid for the dresses,' she wailed.

Over the months Maria's situation grew worse and worse.

'What can I do for her?' Jackie prayed over and over again.

Then she realised the answer to her prayers. Taking her oboe out of its case, she played it for the last time. It sold for exactly the amount of money Maria needed to repay her debt and to free her from slavery to that evil man.

When Jackie Pullinger was a little girl she thought the mission field was a huge green field with a mud hut in the middle.

Her mission field turned out to be very different. It was a vast lawless slum in the middle of Hong Kong. There was no field, there wasn't any grass there at all. There was slime and smells and gangs and drugs and poverty and crime. But there was love too.

Through Jackie many people in the Walled City came to know the love of Jesus, and were loved for the first time in their lives.

FACT FILE
Outer space - at the same time as Jackie Pullinger was stepping off a ship in Hong Kong, man was in a race to travel much further - all the way to the moon!

A Russian, Yuri Gagarin, was the first man in space, when he orbited the earth in April 1961.

Then, after further daring space flights around the earth, an American astronaut, Neil Armstrong, became the first man to set foot on the dry and dusty surface of the moon on 20 July 1969.

Keynote: Jackie was willing to go anywhere for God, even into the Walled City. She was also willing to give up a prized possession - her oboe - to show God's love to someone in trouble.

Learn from Jackie's willingness to go anywhere, do anything and give up everything for God.

Think: Write down a list of the ten things that you value most. When you look at your list you might think you couldn't imagine life without your ten treasures.

What about Jesus? How much does he mean to you? Start to treasure Jesus. Just think about how much he has done for you!

Prayer: Lord Jesus, thank you for everything. Thank you for all the special things you've given me. Most of all thank you for loving me so much that you died for me. Help me not to love anything more than I love you. Amen.

Evelyn Brand

'You have another beautiful daughter,' the nurse told Mrs Harris. 'What a family! Nine children, imagine that!'

Mrs Harris cuddled her newborn daughter and smiled at her husband.

'Have you chosen a name?' the nurse asked.

Without taking his eyes off his new little daughter, Mr Harris answered. 'She's called Evelyn Constance.'

'Nice name,' said the nurse. 'My sister's called Evelyn though we all call her Evie.'

'And will you be called Evie?' Mrs Harris asked the tiny child. It was 1879. By 1880 everyone called her Evie.

Before Evie was very old, another two children had been born into the Harris home. All of them, nine girls and two boys, had the happiest of childhoods in a most beautiful place.

'Chase you to the greenhouse!' was often heard in the summer. And when they came out of the greenhouse to find another game to play there were often red marks on their lips because there were vines in the greenhouse heavy with grapes.

Each summer the gardener grew marrows, and the children watched in amazement as they got bigger ... and bigger ... and bigger still. Sometimes the littlest children could not hold their arms wide enough apart to show how big the biggest marrows were!

'Count up to twenty then come and find us.' But it wasn't always easy to find all the children scattered among the gooseberry and blackcurrant bushes, hiding behind the tall rhubarb or in the fernery where huge fern fronds made splendid hidey places.

Life, however, was not all play for the Harris children, there was school work, church and Sunday School to attend and things to be done for the poor. Although the family was well off, the children knew a lot about poor people. Their mother and father made sure of that.

'Have you put your pennies in the mission box?' the children were asked on Sundays.

'Why do we put money in the box?' the littlest one sometimes asked.

Mother was always ready to explain. 'The poor people in places like India don't know about Jesus so we collect pennies to send people out to tell them.'

That was a very strange thought to the Harris children. In their wildest dreams they couldn't imagine anyone not knowing about Jesus. Didn't everyone's father read them Bible stories? Didn't everyone's mother teach them how to pray? As they grew old enough to understand, they discovered that even in London, not very far from where they lived, there were people who didn't know Jesus.

One of Evie's older sisters married and went to Australia. Evie missed Florrie very much and was delighted when she had to bring her little daughter home for a time. She was still more delighted when her father suggested that she travel back to Australia with Florrie to keep her company. The journey out seemed wonderful to Evie and her time in Australia was too. But it was the journey back that changed her life, for she met a missionary on that boat and God began to call her to missionary service too.

Very soon after she returned to England, Evie heard a missionary speaking about his work in South India. Jesse Brand, a young man home on leave, told about the poverty of the people there, about the disease and starvation, about the dirt and creepy crawlies too. Evie's heart seemed to beat fast. 'Could she go there?' she asked herself. 'Could that be where God wanted her to go?'

When Mr Brand came back to her home for tea, she was too shy to suggest to him that she might go to India. But she knew that she would one day. And that day came quite soon for when Evie made up her mind she went ahead and did things.

'What a noise!' the new arrival in India said to the missionary couple who met her in Madras.

The wife laughed. 'It's a mixture of clattering cart wheels, pounding drums, crows cawing, beggars begging and men shouting out what they have to sell.'

'And if you're wondering what the smell is,' the husband added, 'it's a mixture too, of sandalwood, sweat, jasmine, cow-dung smoke and food.'

Evie struggled to take it all in. 'Could anything be more different from home?' she wondered. But there was no time to be wasted. There was a language to learn and work to be done. Very soon she was visiting Zenana homes with Bible women and deep in study of the language. To her surprise Jesse Brand was in Madras when she arrived. And to nobody's surprise at all the young couple began to fall in love.

In 1913 Jesse and Evie were married and set up home in the hill country among the Tamil-speaking people.

'I so enjoy travelling in this beautiful place,' Evie told her new husband, as they climbed onto their horses for a three day long journey to visit several villages. While Jesse treated the sick, she gathered the women around her and told them in simple Tamil the good news of the Bible.

Just a year after they were married, their little son Paul was born. That meant some changes to their home. Jesse decided that the thick thatched roof, which was home to rats, snakes and other creatures, had to be removed and replaced with corrugated iron. It was a great improvement apart from in the monsoon rains, when it sounded like a whole orchestra of drums beating!

Jesse became well-known for his medical skills though he had only done a one year course in medicine. Sometimes Evie nearly fainted with horror at the patients who arrived at their home. To her they seemed more dead than alive. Jesse didn't fuss, he just did what he needed to do and prayed that God would give healing.

Paul was delighted when his little sister, Connie, was born. The Brand family was complete. Having two children did not stop Jesse and Evie travelling. Leaving Paul and Connie with Christian helpers, they went from village to village as before, caring for those who were sick, making gallons of watery rice for those who were too ill to eat and telling people everywhere they went about the Lord Jesus Christ.

Evie found she had another job too. By 1920 four other children had joined the family. They were Indian children who needed a home and the Brand home was always open to them. But the children who were on Evie's mind at that time were her own for she knew that when the family went back to England on home leave, Paul and Connie would remain there in the care of her family.

'As I stood watching them wave goodbye,' Evie said later, 'something just died in me.'

For the first part of the journey by sea back to India, Evie kept wishing her children were with her. But in the Mediterranean there was such a fearful storm she was glad they were safely home in England.

'We'll write every day,' Jesse had promised the children. And they did. Every evening both Evie and Jesse wrote part of a letter home and, when it was long enough, they sent it off. Paul and Connie were good letter-writers too.

Sadly, letters were all they were ever to have of their father again. Jesse died of fever in 1929 when he was just forty-four years old. It was a heartbreaking letter that told the children that news.

Evie seemed to do enough work for two after Jesse died. That was her way of trying to fill the space he left behind. She visited the village mission stations and held clinics in each one. She inspected schools, gave talks, held prayer meetings, kept the accounts and looked after the Children's Home. Riding Jesse's horse, a rather wild creature of which she'd sometimes been afraid, she picked her way along the trails to distant villages. But help was coming. Ruth, her niece and a doctor, arrived from England and did what she could to assist Evie with her work. The two women lived and worked well together. Evie was especially grateful for her niece when it came time to go on home leave again. It was so hard to face England, to see Paul and Connie, without Jesse at her side.

The children seemed quite grown up to Evie. They had become teenagers in the time they'd been apart. But, much though they loved their mother, there were some things about which Paul and Connie disagreed with her strongly.

'You CAN'T wear that dress!' Connie wailed. 'It came out of Noah's ark.'

Her mother frowned. 'Rubbish. It was my best dress before I went to India, and it has a lot of wear in it still.'

'But people will just laugh at you,' moaned Connie, near to tears.

Connie's aunt came to her rescue. 'Wear this,' she insisted, handing her sister a more modern dress of her own. And, seeing the determination in two sets of eyes, Evie gave in.

Before she left to go back to India, Evie knew that her children loved Jesus for themselves. That gave her courage to say good-bye. Whatever happened to any of them, she was sure they would meet again in heaven.

On her return to India, Evie was given a job in Madras supervising a group of Bible women.

'Time to go,' she said each afternoon, even when the temperature was over 110 degrees. 'I go by rickshaw to the nearer places,' she wrote to Paul and Connie, 'and by bus when I have further to travel. But the buses are so crowded I feel like pulp when I arrive!' She liked trains too, even if they were full of cockroaches!

As the war moved nearer South India, Evie found herself thinking about the bombs that were falling in London, where both Paul and Connie lived. Paul had nearly finished training as a doctor and, as he hoped to work in India, his mother found out about possible jobs for him. In 1947 Paul arrived in the country of his birth, bringing his wife with him.

'If they think I'm going to retire and get under their feet,' Evie told a friend, 'they should think again. I have plans.'

There was a twinkle in her eye and her friend guessed what her plans were.

'I'm going back to the hills again. I'll live in a tiny native hut made of woven bamboo and covered with mud and whitewashed. It'll have a thatched peaked roof like all the other village huts. And I'll be happy there, being a missionary for as long as I can.'

Evie Brand didn't know what it meant to retire. No sooner was she settled in her village hut than she gathered a family of children about her. Some were ill and she nursed them back to health, others were unwanted by their families but never unwanted by Evie.

In 1952, when she was well over seventy years old, Granny Brand, as she was then called, was being carried down a steep hillside on a dholi (chair) with side poles when one of the bearers fell. She lurched forward and landed head first on a rock.

'We need to go back and get help,' the bearers decided.

'No,' Granny Brand insisted, through the pain that pounded inside her. 'We'll go on.'

Miles of being carried in the dholi followed, then a rickety train journey for over a hundred miles and a hot and bumpy bus ride after that. It was a very pained and ill old lady who arrived in hospital in Vellore. Although it took her a long time to recover, that was not the end of Granny Brand's missionary work. Over the years that followed she saw many people trust in Jesus as she shared his story with them.

'That makes it all worthwhile,' she told Paul. 'The work and the pain are all worthwhile if they believe in Jesus.'

Paul knew what she meant. He felt the same.

In 1959, when Granny Brand was nearly eighty, a dream she had had for a very long time came true. Connie, whose home was in Africa, was able to visit India to see her mother. With both of her children beside her, Granny Brand was happy. The hill people, among whom Connie and Paul had been born, made a great celebration to welcome them home.

Evelyn Brand died in India and went home to Jesus in 1974.

FACT FILE

Smell - when she arrived in India, Evie immediately noticed the different smells.

Our sense of smell is controlled by two small areas with many nerve cells, right at the top of the nose.

Humans have a much poorer sense of smell than animals which hunt for prey or have to be on the lookout for enemies.

The human sense of smell also gets tired easily. Have you ever noticed that if you smell a weak smell for several minutes you become unable to smell it at all?

Keynote: Evie began her life in a well-off family in England and ended up in a hut in India, all because of her deep love for Jesus and her love for the Indian people who needed Jesus so much.

Learn from Evie's love for Jesus and how that inspired her to bring his message of love to others.

Think: Evie took the message of Jesus to the people of India, but have you ever thought that you can be a missionary for Jesus right where you are?

The people in your home town need Jesus too so always be on the lookout for ways in which you can share Jesus with them.

Prayer: Lord Jesus, thank you for the people who first told me about you. Help me to love you so much that I will want to share you with others.

Give me the courage to speak up for you whenever I can. Amen.

Joni Eareckson Tada

Tumbleweed trotted through the long grass, then came to the open meadow.

Joni, eleven years old and a rider since she was old enough to sit on a pony, encouraged her horse into a gallop and covered the ground in no time. A sharp tug on the reins slowed the mare down as they reached the little group on the ridge.

'We thought you were never coming,' one of Joni's sisters called, 'but we decided to give you another couple of minutes.'

The four Eareckson girls set out at a trot for their picnic.

'I think this is the most beautiful place in the whole of America,' Kathy said.

Joni agreed. 'I'd hate to live in the town.'

'Being twenty miles away from the bustle suits me fine,' her oldest sister said, 'though I love it when Mum takes us to the shops.'

The other three laughed. 'That's because you want to look at wedding dresses. Wonder why!' Joni spoke for them all. Weddings had been very much in their older sister's mind since she met a certain nice young man.

After their picnic, the four sisters decided to gallop back to the ranch that was their home. As usual the eldest gave the others a few minutes start so that she could keep an eye on them as she rode.

'Really!' she thought as she looked ahead. 'Joni's the limit! She's got Tumbleweed jumping over fences.' Nudging her own horse to move faster, she caught up with her youngest sister. 'Careful!' she called as she neared her, 'You don't want to take a fall!'

Joni laughed and pulled her horse to a trot. 'Tumbleweed wouldn't do that to me.'

'You don't take anything seriously,' the older girl said.

'That's because I never have accidents,' laughed Joni, kicking Tumbleweed into a gallop again.

Her sister grinned and shook her head.

Four years later, when Joni was fifteen years old, she did some serious thinking. At a Christian camp she thought for herself about what the Lord Jesus had done when he died on the cross. Before that she had believed without thinking. A great flood of joy filled her when she realised that Jesus loved her, Joni Eareckson, so much that he died to save her from her sins. Her parents were thrilled when she told them that she was a Christian, for they had prayed for all their daughters since before they were born.

'It's a glorious day,' Kathy said, stretching in the sand.

Their friend Butch threw a beach ball in her direction.

'Joni'll play with you,' yawned Kathy. 'I'm far too busy relaxing.'

Joni and Butch tossed the ball from one to the other, laughing when it went out of reach and racing after it. But the sun was warm and it wasn't long before they collapsed in a tired heap at Kathy's side.

'Time for a swim,' Butch suggested. He looked at Joni and winked. Then he grabbed one of Kathy's hands, Joni took the other and they dragged the girl to the sea. All three ran through the ever-deepening waves and swam back to the shore.

'Like to see a prize-winning dive?' Joni asked.

The other two nodded and waited. Joni's diving was worth watching.

Poised for the dive, Joni took a long breath and jumped. She slid into the warm silkiness of the water in a graceful curve and ......

Butch and Kathy waited to see the curve turn upwards and Joni rise, dripping diamonds of water in the sunshine.

'Joni!' Kathy yelled, instinct telling her that something was wrong. She ran to where her sister hadn't surfaced. Butch followed in a fury of splashing water.

Panic filled Joni when she didn't rise ... when she couldn't rise. She couldn't move ... she couldn't breathe. Her mind was bursting with fear. Her lungs were desperate for air. And still she couldn't rise. Her body and mind screamed for help ... but there was only stillness and a roaring noise in her head that made no sense.

A wave came in, its swell raising the girl a little from the sea-bed.

'Joni!' she heard the echo of Kathy's scream. Then there were strong arms round her, Kathy's arms. Joni saw her sister's eyes. They were bulging with terror. But a cold fear filled Joni. Kathy's arms were round her, she could see that, but she could feel nothing at all. Was her body there? She didn't know. Somehow they got back to the shore.

'Can you feel that?' Kathy begged, touching her sister's leg.

Joni's 'no' was weak.

'Or that?' Kathy's hand was moving up.

'No.'

Then a rush of relief. Joni felt something, it was her sister's fearful, shaking, fingers touching her neck. She tried to reach out to hold Kathy's hand but nothing happened, nothing at all.

There was the screech of an ambulance's brakes. Joni found herself harnessed into a neck brace, lifted by the emergency team into the ambulance and, with siren wailing, the slow procession left the beach for the hospital. Kathy wept noiselessly, clutching her sister's hand in both of hers. But it gave Joni no comfort because she couldn't feel it. Butch followed in the car. He prayed as he drove. Kathy wept all her tears to God. And Joni, seventeen years old and paralysed from the neck down, said the only words that came to her. 'The Lord is my shepherd ... The Lord is my shepherd.' It was 30th July 1967.

The months that followed were terrible. Joni was strapped into a bed that turned her over like a sausage on a barbecue so that she didn't develop sores. For part of each day she was on her back looking at the ceiling, some of the time she was on one or other side facing the walls and for the rest of the day she was suspended from the bed looking at the floor.

'Hi up there,' said Kathy, who was lying on the floor under her sister in order to see her face. 'You won't fall on me, will you?'

Joni looked down. She tried not to cry, but couldn't stop herself. A tear fell from her face and landed on her sister's forehead. Kathy scrambled up and wiped the others that followed. Then she wiped her sister's nose for her.

'You can't imagine what this is like,' Joni whispered, when the tears has stopped. 'Imagine not being able to wipe your nose, or go to the toilet, or even know when you need to go. Imagine having to be fed, having to be washed, having to have your teeth cleaned for you.'

Kathy tried to imagine it, but her mind just couldn't take in the awfulness of it all.

Joni saw the desperation in her sister's eyes. 'No,' she said. 'Don't try to imagine it. It hurts too much.'

As the months passed Joni became more aware of what was happening around her, of other patients who, like her, had broken their necks. Sometimes that was a comfort but mostly it just made the hurt worse to know that other people were as utterly helpless as she was. Her parents, sisters and friends did everything to help but Joni had to travel through her feelings alone.

'Sometimes I remember what it felt like to gallop on Tumbleweed,' she told a school friend. 'I can almost feel the wind in my hair. But then I remember that I'll never ride my chestnut mare again.'

'Try not to think about it if it hurts that much,' her friend suggested.

Joni snapped. 'But how can I not think about it! That's all I have left of a normal life, just memories. And I've nothing to look forward too, all I can do is look back!'

After her friend left, Joni prayed as she'd never prayed before. 'Nobody understands apart from you,' she told the Lord. 'I can only get through the days if you help me. And I just can't imagine how I'll get through life.'

Many years later Joni did some mental arithmetic.

'I've just worked something out,' she told her husband.

'What's that?' smiled Ken Tada, Joni's husband.

'I'm thirty four years old,' she said. 'My accident happened when I was seventeen. That means that for half my life I've been virtually paralysed from the neck down.'

'How does that make you feel?'

Joni thought for a while.

'I guess I feel grateful. After the accident I didn't think I'd live. When I realised I wasn't going to die, I didn't know how I'd cope with living. I spent hundreds of hours just thinking,' she went on. 'I thought I'd be useless, that I'd spend all my life in hospital, that I'd never get married, never travel, never laugh again.'

'Well you thought wrong. Thank God for that.'

Joni nodded.

'There was a song we sang as children. Let's see if I can sing it to you.'

Joni's beautiful singing voice rang out in the evening stillness.

> 'Count your blessings,
> name them one by one.
> Count your blessings,
> see what God has done.
> Count your blessings,
> name them one by one;
> and it will surprise you
> what the Lord has done.'

I do count my blessings sometimes,' she said. 'I actually count them.'

Joni's husband looked at his wife's face, bathed in evening sunlight. She looked beautiful, sitting there in her wheelchair, eyes sparkling as she spoke.

'Would you like to hear some of them?' she asked, just a little shyly.

'I certainly would.'

'You're the first one,' she grinned cheekily, 'though I can't imagine why!' Number two is this beautiful home. I'm so thankful for that. Three is my family and all the people who help so that I can live at home, writing letters, washing, doing my hair, taking down dictation for my books, fetching and carrying things when I need them.'

'That's a lot for one blessing,' her husband laughed. 'What's number four?'

Joni looked serious. 'When I was in hospital I thought I'd never be able to work. Now I have more work than I can keep up with. I never dreamed I'd be a world -wide author. It's such a blessing to write about what God has done in my life and to help others who are going through tough times.'

'And number five?'

'That's my painting,' she nodded in the direction of her easel and palette. 'I wouldn't have believed it was possible to paint holding the brush in my mouth. And to think people actually buy my paintings! Wow! That still amazes me.'

'Any more blessings you want to share?' Joni's husband asked.

'The other thing that really surprises me is the amount of travelling I'm able to do. Just look at my diary for this month. I've got several speaking engagements all over the state, plus one is Washington.

Next month I go to England for a series of meetings there. That's exciting. And the amazing thing is that nobody would ever have heard of me if I hadn't broken my neck. God has brought so many good things out of that terrible accident.'

'Could you bring over my easel, please,' Joni asked. 'That sunset is just begging to be painted.'

Minutes later she was lost in her art. Holding the long handle of the brush in her mouth, Joni mixed the colours of the evening sky on her palette and with swift skilful movements put them on paper. Dark tree branches seemed to reach out of the picture, and her husband, watching her work, could almost feel the warm glow of the bright setting sun on the paper.

'And if you hadn't had your accident, we might not have met,' he thought as he stood behind her stroking her neck so that she could feel his touch.

FACT FILE
Painting - Stone Age artists did the earliest paintings we know of. These paintings were done on the walls of caves.

Joni draws and paints beautifully by holding the brush in her mouth.

Stone Age painters also used their mouths when painting. They blew colour on to the walls through bone tubes. To make the colours stay on they put a kind of glue on the wall.

Right up until A.D. 1400, murals (wall paintings) continued to be one of the main kinds of art.

Keynote: Looking back, it would have been easy for Joni to concentrate on what could have been. Instead she counted her blessings and that made her heart sing.

Learn from Joni's thankful spirit even when things don't

go as you expected. Start by counting your blessings too!

Think: Each time you are tempted to wish for something you don't have, write out a list of the blessings that God has already given you.

Look over the list and you'll find 'it will surprise you what the Lord has done!'

Prayer: Lord Jesus, thank you for everything you have given me. I'm sorry for the times when I am disgruntled and jealous of what others have. Help me to be content.

Thank you especially for your gift of salvation. Amen.

Corrie ten Boom

Corrie's father put on his magnifying eyeglass and looked at the inside workings of the watch. Taking a tiny screwdriver he adjusted a screw the size of a pinhead. Corrie watched him work. He was concentrating so hard he forgot she was there. Although she was only six, Corrie had learned to be very quiet when her father was working on watches and clocks.

Sometimes Corrie wondered what would happen if she let out a great big sneeze. "Atishoo!"

But even when she felt a sneeze twitching inside her nose she always managed to stop herself.

'Would you like to see this through my glass?' Papa ten Boom asked.

Corrie grinned. 'Yes please!' she said, although it was very hard for her to keep his eyeglass in place on her little face. She had to screw her eyes up hard to do it.

'Those are diamonds,' her father told her. 'Can you count how many there are?'

'One, two, three ... four ....five! Who's watch is it, Papa? The lady must be very rich.'

Mr ten Boom smiled. 'Yes, she is very rich.'

'You must be the best watchmaker in Holland,' Corrie said delightedly, 'when rich ladies bring their watches to you. I love being here in the shop with you.'

'I like you being here too,' Father ten Boom said, 'you are quiet as a mouse.'

By the time Corrie had grown up, the Second World War was going on all around her. English and Nazi planes often fought overhead. One night, when the planes were so noisy that Corrie and her sister Betsie couldn't sleep, they went down the twisting stair of their quaint Dutch house and had a cup of tea together. When Corrie went back to bed a long piece of shrapnel lay on her pillow.

'If I'd been asleep it would have killed me,' she told her sister.

Betsie nodded. 'God must have saved you for a reason,' she said.

Corrie, who loved the Lord Jesus very much, agreed. 'But what can the reason be?' she asked. 'I wish I knew.'

It was not long before she found out.

A few months later the ten Boom family discussed the war as they ate their rye bread and Gouda cheese.

'The Nazis are insisting that all Jewish people wear a yellow star, a Star of David,' Betsie said. 'But I don't understand why.'

Papa ten Boom looked very serious. 'Nor do I, but it makes me afraid for them. You don't mark people out for nothing.'

And he was right. The following week Corrie heard Nazi soldiers saying terrible things to young Jewish boys just because they were wearing yellow stars. Then there was word that Jewish men were being taken away to prison camps. But worse was to come. One day Corrie saw Jewish families being pushed on to a lorry and driven away. She knew in her heart that they would never come home again.

'Precious Jesus,' she prayed that night, 'isn't there anything I can do for these poor people?' As Corrie lay in bed that night, she remembered that Jesus was a Jew, and that made her want to help them even more.

'I've an idea,' Mama ten Boom told her daughters after they had seen another lorryload of Jews driven away. 'Our house is such a funny place, with twisting stairs and tiny rooms, attics and underfloor spaces...'

Nollie, Corrie's other sister, interrupted. 'I was thinking the same. We could hide Jews here!'

Corrie and Betsie looked at each other.

'It's like a rabbit warren,' Betsie said. 'We used to play hide and seek when we were girls and sometimes it took ages even for us to find each other!'

Corrie's heart beat fast. 'Was this what God wanted her to do?' she wondered.

The ten Booms made plans. They fixed an alarm bell upstairs so that if any Nazis came into the shop intending going upstairs to search the house, whoever was in the shop could warn the family and any Jews who were there. They would have just two minutes to disappear into one of the many hidey-holes.

'I'm worried about one thing,' Nollie said, when the preparations were nearly done.

'Will children be able to be quiet if they're hidden under the floorboards or in one of the attics? The dust might make them sneeze.'

Every face in the room took on a worried expression apart from Corrie's. 'Yes,' she said firmly. 'They'll be quiet, and they won't sneeze.'

'What makes you so sure?' Betsie asked.

'When we were girls,' Corrie reminded her sisters, 'we were quiet as mice when Papa was working on watches. When we needed to sneeze we stopped ourselves. And our lives didn't depend on it.'

Many Jews were saved because of the ten Boom family but there were hairy moments. One day the whole family and several 'guests' were sitting round the kitchen table when a window cleaner climbed up his ladder and started to clean the outside of the window! One of the Jews thought quickly. 'Start singing Happy Birthday,' he whispered, ' then they'll think we're having a party.' And that's what they did. They all sang Happy Birthday to Papa ten Boom and they never did find out if the window cleaner had just come to the wrong house or if he was a German spy!

But the Nazis eventually discovered the 'safe house' and the ten Booms were arrested, separated and put in prison. It seemed ages before they heard news of each other. One day Corrie got a coded message that all the watches in the cupboard were safe. She knew that meant that the Jews who were hidden in her home when it was raided had got away safely. Corrie was thrilled and she poured out her thanks to God. But the next news she heard broke her heart. Papa ten Boom had died.

'Get dressed and pack your things!' yelled the guards early one morning. The prisoners looked at each other with a mixture of hope and terror. Corrie prayed while she struggled into her clothes.

Guards herded the prisoners into buses and vans outside the prison. But it was not long before they knew they were not being released and sent back home. The buses and vans drew up outside the railway station and the prisoners were dragged off like animals.

That was when it happened. Corrie saw Betsie! She edged her way to her sister without attracting the guards' attention and they clung together. Betsie could just hear Corrie above the noise of the rest of the prisoners. 'Praise the Lord!' she was saying. 'Praise the Lord!'

When an engine pulling cattle trucks stopped at the platform, men, women and children were shoved aboard until they were pressed against each other like sardines in a tin. Corrie and Betsie linked arms so they weren't pushed apart. They talked and talked about what had happened to them during their time apart. And they cried too, especially when they thought about Papa ten Boom.

'We're going to Germany,' a man shouted above the noise. 'We're passing near my home and it's on the way to Germany.'

A woman's voice wailed. 'What'll they do to us there? What'll they do to our children?'

'Nobody ever comes back from Germany,' someone said darkly.

And everyone thought he was speaking the truth.

'I need the toilet,' a child's voice cried.

There was a sudden silence in the carriage.

It was a tearful mother's voice that answered her child, 'You'll just have to do it where you are.'

And everyone in the carriage hoped they would arrive in Germany before they too needed the toilet and had to do it just where they were.

Corrie and Betsie were taken to Ravensbruck, one of Hitler's notorious concentration camps. There they were treated like animals. Each day they had to parade naked in front of the guards, even in the very coldest weather. There was no mercy in the Ravensbruck guards.

'I can't begin to work out how many people are here,' Corrie said one day to her sister.

Betsie couldn't either. 'But I do know something,' she said. 'There must be ten rats for every person.'

'And a hundred fleas,' her sister added.

'I thank God for the fleas,' Betsie said. 'I thank him every single day for the fleas.'

Corrie knew what she meant. The Nazi guards didn't like fleas so when the fleas were especially bad in a hut they didn't go in as often.

'Why didn't God let us go on helping the Jews?' Corrie wondered aloud one day.

Betsie knew the answer to that question. 'Because he had work for us to do here and we'll not do it by being sorry for ourselves.'

Her sister knew that was true. There was so little they could do in the concentration camp but in a place like that little things meant such a lot. Corrie and Betsie looked for ways of helping their fellow prisoners. It's hard to imagine but they even tried to hold birthday celebrations, especially for the young girls there. They cared for sickly children to let mothers rest, and they did what they could for those who were ill and dying. There was love even in Ravensbruck.

'You're so thin,' Corrie told her sister as winter came round, 'and you're shivering with cold.'

'There's nobody here overweight,' Betsie said. Then she smiled. 'And you'd better call out the engineer for the heating seems to have broken down!'

'How like Betsie to try to joke,' Corrie thought. 'Even here. Even now. Even though she's terribly ill.'

Betsie went into a spasm of coughing. But nobody, apart from Corrie, noticed for coughing was the normal background noise in the hut.

As long as she was able, Betsie held Bible studies and little prayer groups. 'That's the best help we can be here,' she often told her sister. 'We don't know how long any of us will live so it's important that we're ready to die.'

Sometimes Corrie prayed that Betsie would get better but other times she prayed that her sister would die and go from the horrors of Ravensbruck into the wonder and beauty of heaven. And that is what happened. Betsie didn't get better. Jesus took her home to himself.

Not long after Betsie died, Corrie was released from the concentration camp. Before she left, she had to sign a form saying that she had been well-treated there and that she had kept in good health. But Corrie was so ill that she was taken straight to hospital. When she was there, she looked in a mirror and didn't recognise herself. Time passed and she recovered enough to go home.

'Do you still have work for me to do?' she asked God often in her prayers. And he did. Corrie opened a home in Holland where other victims of the war came for help and for peace.

One day, a long time later, a man spoke to Corrie after a church service. He had been a guard at Ravensbruck. 'Isn't it wonderful that Jesus has washed my sins away,' he said, holding out his hand to shake hers. So many things went though Corrie's mind. Had he forced her to parade naked? Had he laughed at poor dear Betsie when she coughed herself sick? For a minute her arm seemed glued to her side. Then she prayed a quick silent prayer and God filled her heart with forgiveness. Corrie ten Boom took the man's hand in hers and shook it warmly. And that was a miracle.

FACT FILE
World War II - the Second World War lasted from 1939 to 1945. The Netherlands, where Corrie lived, was attacked by the Nazi army in May 1940 and the country was overrun in four days.

The Dutch underground movement bravely resisted Nazi rule. But more than 100,000 Dutch Jews died in concentration camps and nearly 500,000 Dutch people were sent to work in Germany.

After a terrible winter of famine and cold in the west and heavy fighting in the east, the Nazi forces in the Netherlands surrendered in May 1945.

Keynote: Corrie and her family suffered so much that it would have been easy for Corrie to become bitter and angry. But God gave her real peace in her heart and the ability to forgive those who had been her enemies.

Remember the even greater miracle that Jesus can forgive your sins.

 Think: Maybe you feel you have the right to hate some people because of what they've done. But hatred will make your heart cold and bitter.

It won't be easy but ask God to help you to forgive them and start praying for them too.

 Prayer: Lord Jesus, thank you for being willing to forgive me when I have sinned against you so many times. Help me to forgive others and even to learn to love my enemies as you tell me to do. Amen.

Author Information:
Irene Howat

Irene Howat is an award-winning author and poet who lives in Scotland. She has published many biographical books for all ages and is particularly well-known for her biographical material. She has written many books about the lives of different Christians from around the world. She has also written an autobiographical work entitled: *Pain My Companion*.

Quiz

How much can you remember about these ten girls who changed the world?

Try answering these questions to find out ...

ISOBEL KUHN

1. Isobel went to China, but what was the name of the people she worked with>?
2. What was the name of the special school that John and Isobel ran in the wet season?
3. What were the names of Isobel's children?

ELIZABETH FRY

4. Who was the American gospel preacher that Elizabeth listened to one day?
5. What did Elizabeth give the prisoners before they were transported?
6. How many women were crammed into four rooms at Newgate prison?

AMY CARMICHAEL

7. Which country was Amy from?
8. What colour were Amy's eyes?
9. Where did Amy go as a missionary?

GLADYS AYLWARD

10. How did Gladys travel to China?
11. Where did Gladys work when she came to China?
12. How long did it take Gladys and the children to trek across the mountains to safety?

MARY SLESSOR

13. Where did Mary work as a child?
14. What area of Africa did Mary go to?
15. Before Mary came along, what had the African people done when twins were born?

CATHERINE BOOTH

16. Why did Catherine have to stay in bed for a year?
17. What was the name of the organisation founded by Catherine and William Booth?
18. What was the name of the hall that they opened in one of the poorest parts of London?

JACKIE PULLINGER

19. What was the first musical instrument that Jackie played as a child?
20. What was the name of the area of Hong Kong that Jackie went to work in?
21 Which treasured possession did Jackie sell to pay off a young girl's debts?

EVELYN BRAND

22. What was Evelyn's nickname as a child?
23. Which part of India did Evelyn and her husband work in?
24. Which of Evelyn's children trained as a doctor and returned to work in India?

JONI EARECKSON TADA

25. What was the name of Joni's horse?
26. What had Joni been doing when she became paralysed from the neck down?
27. How does Joni draw and paint?

CORRIE TEN BOOM

28. What job did Corrie's father do?
29. During the war, what did the Nazis insist that all Jewish people wore?
30. What was the name of the concentration camp that Corrie was sent to?

How well did you do?

Turn over to find out ...

ANSWERS

1. The Lisu people.
2. Rainy Season Bible School.
3. Kathryn and Danny.

4. William Savery.
5. A Bible and a sewing kit.
6. 300.

7. Northern Ireland.
8. Brown.
9. India.

10. By train.
11. At an inn for muleteers.
12. Twelve days.

13. In a jute mill in Dundee.
14. Calabar.
15. They killed the babies and sent the mother away.

16. She had a problem with her spine.
17. The Salvation Army.
18. The People's Mission Hall.

ANSWERS

19. A radiator.
20. Hok Nam - the Walled City.
21. Her oboe.

22. Evie.
23. The south of India.
24. Her son, Paul.

25. Tumbleweed.
26. Diving into the sea.
27. By holding the brush or pencil in her mouth.

28. He was a watchmaker.
29. A Yellow Star - the Star of David.
30. Ravensbruck.

Start collecting this series now!

Ten Boys who used their Talents:
ISBN 978-1-84550-146-4
Paul Brand, Ghillean Prance, C.S.Lewis,
C.T. Studd, Wilfred Grenfell, J.S. Bach,
James Clerk Maxwell, Samuel Morse,
George Washington Carver, John Bunyan.

Ten Girls who used their Talents:
ISBN 978-1-84550-147-1
Helen Roseveare, Maureen McKenna,
Anne Lawson, Harriet Beecher Stowe,
Sarah Edwards, Selina Countess of Huntingdon,
Mildred Cable, Katie Ann MacKinnon,
Patricia St. John, Mary Verghese.

Ten Boys who Changed the World:
ISBN 978-1-85792-579-1
David Livingstone, Billy Graham, Brother Andrew,
John Newton, William Carey, George Müller,
Nicky Cruz, Eric Liddell, Luis Palau,
Adoniram Judson.

Ten Girls who Changed the World:
ISBN 978-1-85792-649-1
Corrie Ten Boom, Mary Slessor,
Joni Eareckson Tada, Isobel Kuhn,
Amy Carmichael, Elizabeth Fry, Evelyn Brand, Gladys
Aylward, Catherine Booth, Jackie Pullinger.

Ten Boys who Made a Difference:
ISBN 978-1-85792-775-7
Augustine of Hippo, Jan Hus, Martin Luther,
Ulrich Zwingli, William Tyndale, Hugh Latimer,
John Calvin, John Knox, Lord Shaftesbury,
Thomas Chalmers.

Ten Girls who Made a Difference:
ISBN 978-1-85792-776-4
Monica of Thagaste, Catherine Luther,
Susanna Wesley, Ann Judson, Maria Taylor,
Susannah Spurgeon, Bethan Lloyd-Jones,
Edith Schaeffer, Sabina Wurmbrand,
Ruth Bell Graham.

Ten Boys who Made History:
ISBN 978-1-85792-836-5
Charles Spurgeon, Jonathan Edwards,
Samuel Rutherford, D L Moody,
Martin Lloyd Jones, A W Tozer, John Owen,
Robert Murray McCheyne, Billy Sunday,
George Whitfield.

Ten Girls who Made History:
ISBN 978-1-85792-837-2
Ida Scudder, Betty Green, Jeanette Li,
Mary Jane Kinnaird, Bessie Adams,
Emma Dryer, Lottie Moon, Florence Nightingale,
Henrietta Mears, Elisabeth Elliot.

Ten Boys who Didn't Give In:
ISBN 978-1-84550-035-1
Polycarp, Alban, Sir John Oldcastle
Thomas Cramer, George Wishart,
James Chalmers, Dietrich Bonhoeffer
Nate Saint, Ivan Moiseyev
Graham Staines

Ten Girls who Didn't Give In:
ISBN 978-1-84550-036-8
Blandina, Perpetua, Lady Jane Grey,
Anne Askew, Lysken Dirks, Marion Harvey,
Margaret Wilson, Judith Weinberg,
Betty Stam, Esther John

CHRISTIAN FOCUS PUBLICATIONS

Christian Focus | Christian Heritage | CF4K | Mentor

Christian Focus Publications publishes books for adults and children under its four main imprints: Christian Focus, CF4K, Mentor and Christian Heritage. Our books reflect our conviction that God's Word is reliable and Jesus is the way to know him, and live for ever with him.

Our children's publication list covers pre-school to early teens. We also publish personal and family devotional titles, biographies and inspirational stories that children will love.

From pre-school board books to teenage apologetics, we have it covered!

Christian Focus Publications Ltd,
Geanies House, Fearn, Ross-shire,
IV20 1TW, Scotland,
United Kingdom.
www.christianfocus.com

CF4·K
Because you're never
too young to know Jesus